MIND CONTROL

MIND CONTROL

The Invisible Forces

Joseph M. Daeges

ISBN-13: 9781548691202
ISBN-10: 1548691208
Library of Congress Control Number: 2017910777
CreateSpace Independent Publishing Platform
North Charleston, South Carolina

DEDICATION

We started and funded the women's movement so we could tax both sexes. That way we could put women to work and take their children control.

DAVID ROCKEFELLER

The synthetic solution to these conflicts can't be introduced unless those being manipulated take a side that will advance the Pre-Determined agenda.

GEORG WILHELM FRIEDRICH HEGEL

The truth is in camouflage. It is for us to discern where realities versus lies take root. Joseph Goebbels once said, "A lie told once remains a lie but a lie told a thousand times becomes the truth." I dedicate this book to anyone who has intentions to make this world a better place. If every one of us used his or her abilities to expose negative mind control and to explore the benefit of common sense to create vital laws, we could protect freedom. I am sure we would benefit from acting as a team to defeat any evil root that causes chaos and disorder in our society.

Secret agendas and personal gains do not have a place in a free society. The only agenda we can agree upon in a free society is the freedom of expression. No one is perfect, but if we use past experiences for the growth of our society, we will conquer hate and create a society of peace and order.

TABLE OF CONTENTS

INTRODUCTION

A single death is a tragedy. A million deaths are a statistic.

JOSEPH STALIN

The world will not be destroyed by those who do evil, but by those who watch them without doing anything.

ALBERT EINSTEIN

*M*IND CONTROL: THE *invisible forces* is not a conspiracy theory. This book is trying to shed light on the personal agenda and global indoctrination through the medium of mind control. The personal views of the author regarding mind control are written with the intention to unveil where the idea of globalization takes root. I am sure the subject of "mind control" alone will provoke many controversies and will perplex many. Do not be afraid to face controversy regarding mind control. In some cases, conspiracy theories make their way definitively into our society. Inspired by the teamwork of a healthy society, we will be able to fight negative exploitation of mind control. If we choose to stay idle and adopt an indifferent attitude, we will surrender and become prisoners of a negative field of exploitation from evil individuals who explore mind control.

There are five kinds of professional creepy liars we face in a negative mind control environment:

1. *Sociopathic liars* make up incredible lies and seem to believe them, and that is why they can sell them so well.
2. *Habitual liars* lie to get themselves out of trouble or responsibility. They lie to keep themselves safe and to survive. Their favorite line: "I didn't do it."
3. *Sporadic liars* tell the truth most of the time but sometimes feel the need to embellish. By only lying "once in a while," they can excuse themselves.
4. *Sloppy liars* like to make up stories. They do it for the attention.
5. *White lies* are usually regarded as harmless and sometimes even helpful. They might include flattery or telling a lie to make someone feel good. But lies are still lies.

Stop making excuses and stop lying—face the truth; admit the truth.

"You can't help a liar."

1

WHAT IS MIND CONTROL?

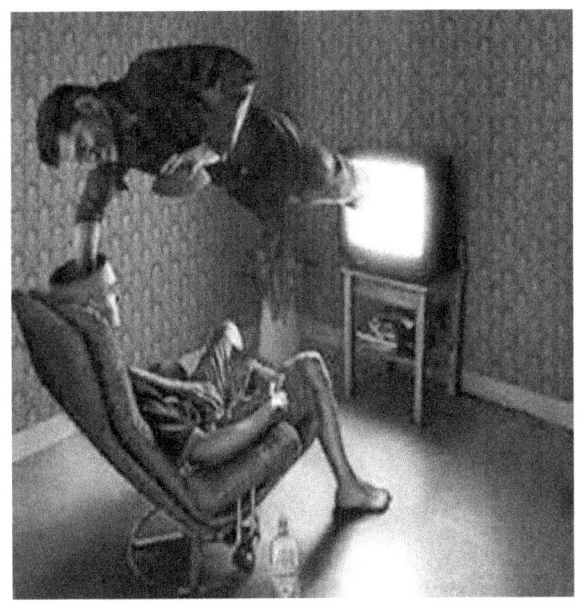

MIND CONTROL OCCURS when one individual or a group of individuals have been forced to surrender their person to a dictated regime or personal belief that fundamentally influences their ability to think and make choices. While there are many forms of mind control, voluntary mind-set is the fault of the adult individual who blindly accepts a belief system or lifestyle. Some individuals will accept brainwashing as an easy way out of their daily activities or responsibilities. For others, it will be a secret abstraction to justify some personal way for guiding toward their vision and journey to acquire perfection.

This author sets out to reeducate the reader on his or her path. For the sheep, it becomes the only way to survive and to adjust among their newly controlled society. Reeducation takes many forms of repeat occurrences and manipulative tactics. For example, a leader of mind control, with twisted knowledge and oratory skills, could categorize his sheep.

Presuming adeptness on the part of the chieftain, the followers will become convinced that the leader has answers and knows how to promote peace. From that moment on, the master of mind control engulfs the souls of his or her followers. Due to mind-control mechanisms, a leader will deceive his or her followers into thinking that his or her behavior is acceptable and loveable. It is evident that mind control influences those who live under a dictatorship. Mind control results in an opportunity to take away individual freedom and to redistribute it as the founder pleases, whether in times of peace or in times of disruption and chaos.

Most of the time, mind control is manipulated in order to seem to favor the individual. But in some cases, a group of individuals is needed to create an environment where individualism is considered unreachable. The only way to access knowledge is to be under the surveillance of a commander who presents himself or herself as the ultimate authority. In a society, some are vested with knowledge about and experience with education and family. When the time arrives to use mind control, these individuals are dying for control and to gain momentum. History has proven to us the many circumstances under which evil came about when individuals hungered for more power.

Today more than ever, we are pressured under a solid foundation, created over centuries, that dictates how individuals should live. Not everyone in a society will fall for the promises of individuals who present themselves as saviors. Instead, they will study the downside of succumbing to the trap of mind control. These individuals become enemies specifically because they label themselves as morally stronger than the mind-controlling powers of the mastery.

In order to create the perfect environment for mind control, the government and the individual both have to use a set of ideas. My intent is not to blame anyone or any government agency but simply to expose both the dangers and the benefits of mind control. Yes, in many cases mind control is a doorway toward prosperity, knowledge, and the development of a balanced individual. It is unfortunate that we also face exploitation and abuse, even in a good environment where mind control is needed. One bad apple is more than enough to spoil the positive effects of mind control.

Why are so many inclined to follow blindly without asking questions or seeking advice? Why are people afraid to step outside the norms of society? There are multiple answers to these questions, because at the end of a day, mind control only exists because individuals make choices.

Mind control gains power because individuals form society. For some in society, mind control is easy to defeat, and for others it becomes a battlefield. Mind control structures the environment of our own existence, though we may not realize this all the time.

The Creator of this universe set forth the rules and regulations that dictate nature. While mind control is necessary when abusing power, true mind control is not acceptable. Mind control appears in our society with many faces, beliefs, traditions, cultures, and perceptions. We are part of a machine that makes it impossible to escape the wrath of evil-minded individuals dying for power, money, and sex. Mind control takes over a sick individual more quickly than a healthy one who would be morally strong enough to battle coercion. Nothing works better than an ideology that is well calculated by an individual pretending to be well educated but who is, in actuality, shallow and empty.

Empty promises lure and provoke some individuals to fall for the evil mind-set. These individuals will surrender to a charlatan promising a situation where salvation or happiness will finally be miraculously bestowed upon them. These individuals, freely or under pressure, will become bait and will be used by these crooked monster mind-sets to continue their evilness. We do have a need for orderly and proper ways of living, which are well defined on the chart of human rights and societal norms. These rights are guaranteed to each of us from the day we see the light of this universe.

For those individuals whose instincts are guided by the desire to control and exploit, this becomes a right for them to take away independence from their future subordinates. These twisted mind-control individuals will formulate and dictate many reasons why their possessions should only abide by their dictated rules and regulations. Anything and everything outside of their presenting ideologies becomes dangerous, stupid, and out of line. Coercions are masterly used to ensnare future projected possessions from a stance of view of a perverted mind-control freak individual.

Once in the realm of mind control due to coercion, individualism does not exist. No one under the spell of mind control has the knowledge or ability to regulating. This is made clear at the start of a situation where evil individuals use mind control, and the sheep are forced to surrender everything. This means that the way the sheep dress, eat, sleep, and go about their daily routine is dictated. Everything has momentum and a purpose dictated by masters who use coercion to acquire and possess individual dreams.

This is unfortunate, but throughout history we have come in direct contact with good mind control and pure evil mind control to remind us mind control can be a negative tool. History also teaches us that persuasion works with precision, especially in a controlled environment. Individuals who are unfortunately guided by poor judgment find themselves free, or at times forced, to live under the rules and dictation and demand of mind control domination.

Not all mind control situations are bad, individuals who conclude mind control is evil believe erroneous lies. We just have to recognize the dangers and symptoms of negative mind-control situations. There are many organizations where mind control is used to demolish instead of construct positive avenues. Since World War II, how many experiments have been performed upon individuals and families? Only the ones who have freely chosen to exploit the phenomenon of mind control can answer this question. Most likely, the one who paved the way to enter into the heart of mind control died long ago, but the evil didn't die with him or her.

Others have chosen to continue to pursue fundamentalist ideologies to develop more control upon the universe. This is like a drug: the more you take in and justify the exploitation, the more you make excuses for a negative situation. Don't be a slave to your desires and emotions; instead, become a grower of good ethical seeds in your mind and heart. It is unfortunate to surrender the power of your mind to another source—you open the door to imposters, and their ideologies begin to control your inner self.

Persuasion underlies the will to conquer any individual who feels pressure to adhere to strict authority. This becomes the one key played with such precision that anyone could fall for the deception (or benefit because not everyone is evil by nature). There are persuasions that are noble and legitimate, such as those coming from the loving hearts of parents, friends, church members, and family. A good example is the mark of the positive avenue directed by the vigilance and love of a person who hopes to make a good impact on the recipient.

There will always be a need for positive mind control in order to open doors to independence instead of creating an environment of dependency. One of the most obvious traits of negative mind control is if the recipient has only one choice and is forced into submission. Evil trends toward controlling the target while referring his would be a continuation of mind control. By doing so, the outsider becomes a mentor, and the insider becomes a voluntary slave. This is where the evil mind-set of individual exploitation searches to entrap the sheep for good, to the point where the victims think the evil individual is their master, and they act for him.

Mind control has two major outcomes depending on different personalities or goals: set to do good or set to do evil. There are many forms of mind control and personality traits that send signals of dominance. For some abusers, their major mind control is their regard for others. Such regard will be preceded by fear, even if those fears are not realistic. Nevertheless, because of the sense of dependency instilled in the recipient of mind control, he or she cannot distinguish between real and unreal.

Most of the time, an individual who is capable of being voluntarily deceived is not in control of his or her personal affairs. This is because of the choice to abandon one's sanity to the will of the mind controller. They act in accordance with their chosen savior, master, or lord, who will forever become entwined in their twisted personality. It is very hard to break away after being exposed to a mind-control environment at a young age; nothing makes sense, and the right to be an individual is taken away.

As these children grow, the biggest barrier is fear. These individuals who were raised in a negative mind-control atmosphere learn not to give themselves credit for a job well done. Also, as they get older, due to mental isolation and their parents' choices, they are reluctant to snap out of a situation where mind control dictates all their activities. Children who are exposed to negative mind control are brave when they consider reforming the thoughts they received from being brainwashed.

The negative effects of brainwashing explain how totalitarian regimes appeared to systematically indoctrinate their people. False ideologies guard and groom mental walls so that the recipients will not have control over their own thoughts. The younger the victims, the more likely they will never access their own individual thoughts.

In the view of a dictator, family does not exist. Although in most cases, this same dictator has been given the chance to experiment with the benefits of belonging to a family. The moral destruction of family follows with physical separation and the arbitration of legitimate right in the face of true freedom.

Mind control could also be used for good behavior. Not everyone has the mentality of a sociopath or a control freak, but it is good to remember that the more power you have, the more you ask for and wish for. If there weren't any laws and regulations, individual lives could be in danger. For example, not obeying a red light while driving a car could end someone's life.

Many good behaviors are expected when everyone submits to and corroborates with existing laws and regulations. However, the slippery side of mind control and its influence must be scrutinized to expose anyone who abuses this natural phenomenon. One bad apple in an authoritative position could easily spoil the bunch. Sometimes a bad apple catches us off guard or takes us by surprise, and so we are forced to ask, "Why do more and more individuals continue to not trust authorities, law enforcement officials, and the justice system?"

The one delegate who serves the role of public servant might be the only one who can answer this question. Mind control is a system that has been studied for centuries, especially during World War II. The Maoist government in China used this system to transform individual thinking into a reactionary, imperialist mind-set of "right thinking." Today, with technology far more advanced since World War II, it has become so much easier to program individuals. The meaning of the term punned on the Taoist language is "cleansing and washing the heart and mind."

Why is mind control not abusing? Most likely, individuals forced into mind control find themselves violating their legitimate ability to denounce, and sometimes they even betray their own country. Also, why do some authorities use mind control in experiments to program an mentally heal individuals? The fact is, the studies of this broad orison of mind control and immediate extension control have been secretly researched for a long time. Why is their aim to unveil all the mysteries that mind control has to offer? This is a question that does not relate to everyone, only to those trusted by the general public and given the charge to maintain order in society.

There are some very interesting facts found in studying the match up that occurred after World War II. Adolf Hitler and Joseph Stalin were two of the most notorious individuals who were not afraid to rule and control by force and rarely by kindness. They were also dictators groomed to impose order into a society or group of individuals. Most of the time, these individuals, chosen by the elite, are born and raised dictators. Mind control has done some tremendous good for our society, but nevertheless, we have to remember all the disasters dictators have created. We also have to remember the victims who struggle even today because of experiments in mind control programs.

With the advanced technology of today, it is nothing for a profiteer to create a master plan in order to gain prosperity, power, and control. Technology is a tool that lays the perfect groundwork for experiments that, most of the time, appear to be the solo work of one party and not a well-executed plan. Nothing works better to present an illusions, just like movies in the theater, where the story on the screen occupies the minds of individuals. Fiction combined with facts blend with precise artifacts and collusion to set up believable evidence, resulting in mind control. So, a majority of individuals trust the daily report they see on their screen while sitting comfortably at home on their couch. Fiction creates illusion, and persuasion immediately follows.

2

RULERS USING MIND CONTROL

Who is Promoting?

- Governor
- Speaker of the House
- Construction firms
- Developers
- People who benefit from the taxes
- Chambers of

THERE ARE MANY parties and groups that benefit from having a director who uses mind control. There are also situations where we become the author of our own mind control. For example, when a bad habit becomes an obsession to the point where individuals become slaves of pleasure that interfere with every aspect of life. This obsession is provoked by such means as advertisements, radio shows, indoctrination, and the influence of close friends. There is a long list of causes and durations of many types of mind control that are poised to program the minds of individuals. Once the news media or radio shows promote ideology about something as simple as lighting up a cigarette, the consequences are hard to reverse.

There was a tremendous effort on the part of television programs in the sixties to advertise cigarettes to the point where every actor was encouraged to smoke on screen. At the time, it was believed that nothing bad would come from smoking. Now, in our day, the same instrument is used to demonize the same product and demonstrate how it causes lung cancer. Individuals become unable to say, "I will stop promoting my own death by smoking." Instead, the market goes around, and the sheep fall victim to their own enemy while the news media and radio shows condition their brain.

I do not intend to make an argument for or against smoking. Rather, I want to demonstrate how mind control can promote a product and then demonize the same product. This everyday propaganda reminds us how frail we really are and how easy it is to outsource and control our minds. There are also other ways in which we become our own worst enemy. Let's face it: alcohol is it, because we are the product of imagination.

The more power you give to one individual to create a situation where everything is allowed and nothing is bad, the more devastating the consequences. Then again, there is nothing wrong with enjoying a margarita or a good glass of beer or wine. The list could go on to the point where we don't know where to stop. The mind is now controlled under the influence of the alcohol-induced boost; the more you consume, the more you think you need to reach a certain point. Mind control takes many forms and shapes, depending on where your mind has its attention, resulting in a disregard for the consequences of certain actions.

Some authors of mind-control studies have shown how ideologies can, at first glance, seem innocent and legitimate. These are the powerful moments of mind control. These individuals become professionals in setting up failure and even setting up deadly situations. Everyone is familiar with World War II, a situation where a group of greedy individuals used exploitation and dependency to control the minds of others.

These individuals had chosen to disregard the nature of individualism to create an atmosphere of control— a moment that became experimental in our own history. Many countries have used mind control to target "enemies" during times of confrontation, leading to worldwide wars. Many evil tactics have been adopted and created to control and force prisoners of war into submission, to the point where they are no longer aware of their existence. We all know that waterboarding, starvation, and isolation have all been used to break down strong personalities.

These strong personalities, who had sworn to never divulge sensitive information under any circumstances, eventually succumbed to the torrent of pressure imposed on their minds to finally reveal their secrets. Mind control is a powerful moment of truth that can be used to construct or demolish anyone. We are all the products of a form of mind control: from the day of our arrival here on Earth, we have been taught what life is, how to preserve it, and how to follow its natural laws. We all have a morning and a night, a sun during the day and a moon at night.

We all have to eat and drink in order to survive, and if we are deprived or choose not to comply with this natural mind-set, death is inevitable. We are set up with many faces and personalities, yet we have to follow our own individual routines and lifestyles. However, the quality of our lives depends on our own disposition and vision as to what we consider important. We all function the same way, but we are in control of what and whom we choose to be programmed by.

World War II was not only a physical duel but also the beginning of open warfare on an individual's mental capacities and fragilities. During World War II, brainwashing was covered up to the point that no one suspected it existed. Of course, there were some "high dignitaries" (that today we call "government-instructed individuals") who were dying for more power and control. Nothing stands in the way of mind control. For example, the use of lies, promises, critical judgment, and advertisements all convene to control the sheep. With mind control, there is no human flesh or personality because mind control sees the body as "a thing."

Once individuals are labeled as "things," the one who does the labeling becomes the heart of mind control. Once at this level, it is impossible for the "thing" to have emotions or feelings. The one who has succeeded in luring his or her victim, flashing some nice promise of happiness and prosperity, is incapable of distinguishing between a "thing" and a real person. From now on, with his victim hostage, all the mind control master has to do is ensure that the "thing" will not experience a wake-up call. To do so, the usurper employs many tactics to keep the "thing" ignorant and interpreting his or her every word as holy and prophetic.

World War II ignited a vast field of exploitation by the medium of mind control, lasting even up to today, where we are supposedly so far advanced in technology. We are constantly under attack from the Left, then after a while from the Right—Democrat, Republican, Independent, you name it. They have different faces, creeds, and morals, but they share the same goal with the same results. Above all, nothing works better than using advertising by means of the media and the fine art of technology.

Good and evil forces surround us every day, and the phenomenon of mind control is reigning. Every time you turn the television on or simply listen to the news, you are bombarded with multiple ads promoting pills for pain or promised medical miracles. Not only are we spotted by the shadow of an instant fix situation but we are also saturated by mental oppression. Medication "drugs," masterly maneuvered by puppeteers, are the new approach the ones that fit the most during the evolution of the twenty-first century.

This does not mean that all medications are evil and should be avoided, but it points out the tremendous effort on behalf of the ones who control the media in our day. The more power one individual is granted, the more this person will want to remain in power. The power of mind control is by far a domain where our human consciousness (or unconsciousness) is navigated every day. For some, taking advantage of this magnetic field is a given, and for others, falling into the traps set by those who exploit becomes their daily experience.

Like I said earlier, we are also our own subjects of mind control because all of us have, at some point, made a decision that impacted our lives. Our minds are constantly reaching out to new ideas and propositions. Vendors know by experience how easy it is to convince the future by making a deal with a buyer. Really, the only one who benefits from the deal is the vendor because although he claims he is forging a deal, only he possesses the knowledge of how much profit he will have. So, the deal is not entirely fair, but it is considered fair because of the agreement. One is gaining money and one is gaining a "deal."

Mind control is like a signature that seals the deal, where the one who is exploiting never fails to make a profit, and the one who is exploited always comes out short because of not knowing the whole picture. The description of the deal does not necessarily reflect the actual cost of the merchandise, and this becomes the privilege of the seller to exploit the buyer. There is nothing wrong either way; the seller is asking for a price for some good he or she likely never did pay for with the intention of making a profit.

The same scenario appears to be the case when a perverted, corrupted mind-control specialist decides to conduct experiments upon "things" in his or her neighborhood. Since World War II, how many "things" have mysteriously disappeared? Some of these people were important individuals. Mind control regulates every inch of every square foot when it comes time for calculating measurements and consequences. In some fatal situations, a scenario is made to make a murder look like a suicide, a school shooting, a road rage incident, or another type of carnage.

Mind control is becoming more and more up for grabs. The more one succeeds in the field of mind control, the more power is bestowed. Technology is so far advanced that we do not need previous geniuses like Einstein, whose research was most likely guided by mind control. Nevertheless, these geniuses, who lead in knowledge and power today, are the key. More than ever, ascent toward complete control is becoming accessible through the medium of mind control.

Sheep depend on the news media and television, which are controlled by individual influence and knowledge in the field of mind control. Little effort is needed to turn on the radio or the television and retrieve controlled information morning, noon, and evening. Most of the sheep are too busy to read a book about fact versus fiction. But this dependency did not occur in one day; this was the culmination of a process, and it still is a process. Every day new details are being discovered, and unexpected situations arise where information is leaked to the general people.

Rapidly, this leaked information is ridiculed and even declared to be a conspiracy. There is no need to pay attention to hate mongers. The majority of society who believe media and broadcasting sources without a second thought will surrender to the machine of mind control. Some people will investigate but will choose to keep their opinions to themselves because of previous unpleasant experiences.

This is how much mind control has a direct impact upon the society we live in today.

Every day the machine of exploitation bombards us, and every day is a step toward total belief and dependency. The ones who manipulate the news are now in control of our emotions. Expectations replace common sense, leaving a small place for logic. The sheep are guided toward one gold-standard way of living, as if they were living in a moral concentration camp.

Talking about mind control is a special subject, and I do recognize that some of my readers will say, "This book is worse than a conspiracy theory." My questions to you, my reader, are, "How do you define conspiracy theory? Are you just following the mass of sheep who believe with their whole heart what the media puppeteers are saying?" I am amazed to live during this era and witness the devastating effects of negative mind control upon a whole universe.

Hitler would never have succeeded in provoking the whole world to be at war without the collaboration and dedication of secret puppeteers pulling strings. They created the revolutionary idea of mind control at birth—that everyone on Earth would surrender to their mind control, whether by peaceful means or forcible means. Revolution brought the perfect grounds to initiate new laws and regimentation under the cover of restoring order in society. Then and now, we are witnessing the powerful message of mind control all over the universe.

To help the masterly plan of pulling strings, all means are acceptable, even the legitimate pleasures and good times we are entitled to. For example, bars became a way for mind control to erase the sheep's pain and hardship, if only for a short period of time. The pleasure of sport also negatively entraps those who do not need to frequent bars but want to enjoy their legitimate right for a good time. I am not speaking against any sport or legitimate right to pleasure; I am trying to make a connection between our legitimate rights to pleasure and the mind control infesting our daily lives.

Even farmers are not spared from the regimentation of mind control. Different laws and demands have, over time, controlled their every move. The creation of genetically modified organisms (GMOs) is another form of mind control that tells us what we should eat. Global warming, I should really say now "Climate changing" has become a threat because we are putting our planet in severe danger and causing irreparable damage every day. Fertilizer became a severe cause of problems, discovered by the media and its controlled group of puppeteers.

As sanctions are imposed, living becomes harder and harder for citizens who struggle to survive. For the one aware of these criminal activities, he or she is stunned by how these audacities make it possible for mind control to co-exist harmoniously. I am not saying that every authority is corrupt and follows the path of audacity; nevertheless, I want to explain a certain point of view.

This chapter talks about those who are the authors of mind control, and the subject itself reveals an immense field of variety very well used by mind-controlling authorities. A good way to make a criminal activity acceptable is to lie about it and work under cover. For example, Monsanto empoison millions of people by a chemical that does not belong in our food. This chemical called Glyphosate is ending up in processed foods like Cheerios, Ritz Crackers, and Oreos and being consumed by humans across the world. The health of millions of people is on the line. Glyphosate, the main ingredient in round up, is dangerous to human health and should be banned like DDT. The dictionary use for the definition of DDT is Merriam Webster and it is describing as a colorless odorless water-insoluble insecticide C14H9Cl5 that is an aromatic organochlorine banned in the Unite Sate of America that tends to accumulate and persist in ecosystems and has toxic effects on many vertebrates

This product is a cause for why people get:

Fat
Cause birth defect and tumors
Binds needed metals in body and removes them
An antibiotic killing beneficial gut bacteria
Has a possible link to autism?
Link to cancer and others illness
Damage cellular DNA.

The only way this injustice will be corrected is if enough of us stand up and demand that something be done to stop the poisoning of our food supply.

We are living under a spell of mind control because of family traditions paving the way for the next generation. Traditions are legitimate; however, they do not possess a soul. The problem occurs when a soul governs traditions.

Now having said this, I do not want anyone to live in fear and wonder if he or she has been exploited and targeted. Let's face it: authors of mind control are found in all levels of our society. This implies that families are as much puppeteers as those who strive to maintain power through tradition.

In this chapter, I have targeted the many faces and tactics of mind control, and I have exposed how we are forced to abide with and adopt mind control. Just remember, authors of mind control only possess their almighty power to the degree we let them. Authors of mind control appear in other forms and situations because we navigate among regulations, rules, laws, and specific, orderly ways of conducting our daily activities.

We do need to categorize what is considered a legitimate, constitutional right of freedom versus a criminal activity. Criminals have studied every angle of mind control, and its consequences have been studied. The day will come—I hope not soon—when we will be tracked with a microchip. How far will audacity take us? Also, how long will we, as the living generation, let these monsters operate and control us against our will?

Mind control is a very powerful tool because it is found in almost every activity we do every day, from the moment we get to work to the moment we relax at home with our family. Let us recognize the danger and the benefits of mind control. The sooner we face reality, the better things will be for the generations to come. If we scrutinize the writing, we miss the point of the exposé. If we analyze the pros and cons of mind control, we are well placed to face any bad and controlled situations.

3

WHAT DOES MIND CONTROL ACCOMPLISH?

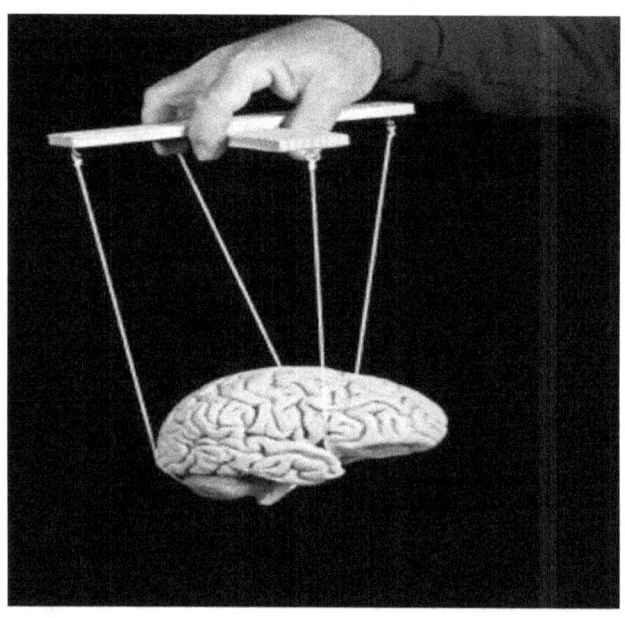

AFTER HAVING EXPLORED some of the sources of mind control, I will move on to the question, "What does mind control accomplish?" The list of negatives and adverse effects could be longer than the list of positives and benefi-cial effects. Nevertheless, I will try to go over the two pos-sibilities equally because I do not want to be influenced by one force more than the other. I know mind control is a vir-tual jackpot that depends upon one move on a game board. For the player, it will be a victory or a disaster.

Let's explore what, in my view, good mind control can accomplish. There are five major outcomes that come springing out of my mind: education, knowledge, experi-ence, endurance, and reliability. In this description, there are the basics of our lives, and the reasons for educating ourselves about positive mind control. Often, we have the tendency to neglect or not acknowledge the good side of things. We have the opportunity to experiment positivizes environment and also destructives conditions.

It is always easier to find negative repercussions from an event than to analyze the big picture in order to discover the hidden positives. While talking about mind control, we do not realize how vulnerable we are to the universe of mind control surrounding us. Nevertheless, good education over centuries of experience bestowed upon generation after generation leads to knowledge—the most precious positive outcome of mind control.

Why is this continuation between generations the most positive aspect of mind control? For me, the answer is simple: one experience is worth more than one unknown situation. From the knowledge of a previous generation's experiences, we now have a good idea how to tackle the obstacles posed by negative mind control. While other good experiences help to promote the outcomes of positive mind control, we all have to make a choice to follow a certain path.

In positive mind control, the essence of common sense, trust, peace, education, and humor flourishes. Positive mind control creates an environment where we learn how to trust each other, while negative comparisons between differences and cultures are eliminated. This is the positive side of comprehension: discovering who we are and what we can achieve, inspired and instructed by the positive trajectory of mind control. Of course, there will be some imperfections; however, we should always try to find positives in imperfections and not allow them to serve as an excuse to not perform with relentless dedication.

We, at our core, have so much to gain from creating an environment of unity. We depend upon each other, although we are very independent. We are the ones who pick and choose who we want to associate with and live with. We are part of this universe, and this universe becomes part of us, with or without our consent, from the day we are old enough to realize we are free to choose. Yes, this whole positive attitude about mind control allows for each individual to strive toward many different outcomes because mind control by itself is incapable of making exclusions.

Why do we have so many negative situations created by refusing to take responsibility and developing a "who cares" attitude? It is always easier to project our problems onto others, but this is not a positive avenue to go down in an effort to handle our responsibilities. It is very important to ensure our future generations are not deprived of their capacity for positive mind control. This would be a disaster for future generations because the less chance you give to a positive avenue, the harder it becomes to create positive benefits.

Education from parents, with the help of the media and immediate friends, is a must while we consider the benefits of positive mind control vested upon our children. It is important for adults to take responsibility to educate from the heart and not let someone else take control of it. It is so much easier to let someone else take control of our responsibilities than to hold ourselves accountable for our actions and decisions. Human nature will always tempt those unaware or careless individuals.

At the end of the day, we harvest the fruit of what we have planted—not only in our personal affairs, but also in the future affairs of generations to come. A good example of positive mind control is when children blindly learn at a young age. Children have a vision of development at an age when they struggle to be independent, such as when they learn to walk and learn other basics of life. Common core values become common strategies. A simple example is harvesting fruit because we can run from mistakes, but we surely cannot hide from their long-term consequences.

Even after we pass away, our children and grandchildren should be able to say, "I have contributed to positive ways of mind control because of my parents' (and also in some cases, my grandparents') positive education and love for me." There are so many benefits to gain from positive mind control. Why not search and promote good avenues from this genial source? It takes one day at a time for this marvelous, magical influence to take solid root for the generations to come. One disposition can create positive rays of mind control that will eventually be the foundation of bright and fruitful descendants.

It is important to consider these positive sides of mind control because we have a tendency to blame bad situations as an excuse for our own negligence. Why not ensure that mind control is used to construct a proud and cheerful morale as a legacy to our own generation? Every moment we spend being a good example works toward the common good of future generations as much as we develop our pride in doing the right thing.

We would have many advances in our society if sheep would wake up from their mental paralysis and partake in their fair share of responsibilities. Eventually, even the radio and media would be forces that allowed us to embrace the positive avenues that mind control offers us. This will be the fruit of a good example versus an attitude of laissez-faire created and maintained by abandoning our future and future generations.

Positive mind control is the ultimate charm that stops hate, and we are finding ourselves by exposing our negligence. Life is the fruit of the efforts individuals make while they create positive moments to be shared and provide momentum for expansion. We all have a unique opportunity to educate ourselves and others about peace, joy, love, and respect as we engage in positive communication.

Let us remember that tomorrow is the consequence of yesterday, and the day after tomorrow will define and eternalize our reputation after we pass from this world. The question we should ask here is, "Would we like to be remembered as loyal and good mind-control educators and experienced individuals who gave it all to create a better world?" I cannot answer this question for you. The only right thing I can do now is to answer this question for myself. If my answer is yes, then the game plan is in my hands, and the tools ready to be used are my disposition and willingness to create a difference.

This simple question seems easy to answer for the responsible individual. The twist is to have all members of this world collaborate with the same amount of courage and pride. We take an oath to our future generations—to give all of our love, courage, and pride to help them tackle this journey while time gives us the opportunity. Mind control is a wonderful tool to solidify what we believe to be weak and to also perfect what we choose while considering the power of mind control.

I made a promise to speak about the positive effects of mind control before elaborating on the negative effects. I hope my readers will realize two things: mind control is not a bad thing, and we must preserve honesty in mind control.

Now let us shift our attention to the devastating consequences of exploitation in the field of mind control. This will contrast with the positives discussed earlier in this chapter. We must let our abilities acknowledge that bad mind control engenders all sources of evil. A society controlled by evil has less freedom and kindness to share. I am not trying to advocate resentful sentiments; instead, I am exploring a way to expose evil.

Bad mind control can be found everywhere we travel and throughout history. This phenomenon has been studied and experimented with since the start of World War II. It became indoctrination, which used education to quench a thirst for power, control, and exigence. Imperialism took root upon the whole world with socialist ideologies to divide and conquer.

The Left prefers to use education as a method to destabilize the Right. This creates a situation where the vulnerable have no choice but to submit to the fighter who still has pride and strength to stand up against tyranny. Since World War II, with the advancements and indoctrinations influenced by television, the world has witnessed the decadence of it in society. Advertisements coming from liberal puppeteers have swamped the heart of every family.

The precise movement of strings by the crooked mind of these puppeteers created this well-orchestrated plan. A handful of individuals declared mental war against the whole universe in order to succeed. Every time the liberal agenda wanted to advance one of their ideologies, they did not hesitate to destabilize their "number-one enemies": family values and traditions. The radio became the source of mind control for those who weren't able to swallow the televisual mind-control setting.

Indoctrination replaced instruction, and knowledge became a privilege, while the imposition of a dictatorship was accepted when coming from a twisted individual mandate. Schools had no choice but to endorse the indoctrination of a whole generation because of carelessness in the previous generation. We are tormented at the hands of a few mind-control master dictators who do not have any sense of honesty or dignity. All that matters are to divide in order to conquer. Sometimes force is required, but the regimes tend to use kindness to cover up their evilness.

Evil mind-control settings accomplish nothing positive; they only destroy and desolate people of value and pride. When evil, maniacal individuals use mind control with no regard or value for other lives, they succeed in imposing their agenda of slavery. Crooks use mind control to create an atmosphere where dependence replaces independence, and no longer are sheep able to function on their own.

Mind control became a drug for the sheep and a harsh reality for the ones who refused to submit to the rule of evil dictatorship. These mind control crooks adopted education as an opportunity to wipe out any good morals among the weak and the sheep. In the process of negotiating peaceful results, the puppeteers pulling the strings were audacious enough to blame morality as the cause of all disorder and misconduct. These hidden manipulators have come to redefine and rewrite their own version of morality.

What was once considered bad and a crime has become a constitutional claim of the right of liberty and freedom of choice. Constitutions become worthless, and patriotism becomes a source for terrorist acts, while the flag of the country burns in bright light. Everything is allowed, and the master puppeteers themselves are the ones who encourage people to submit under their umbrella of what they have defined as freedom. Riots, revolts, and protests become the norms as people come to surrender under the pressure of these crooked freaks capable of devilish mind control.

Mind control has significantly increased in volume, astuteness, and cruelty, resulting in increased exploitation and, above all, unlawful activities. Why are we submerged in so much abuse of power? What insanity led our society to accept and adopt these treatments? This is a long shot at exploring the possibilities versus the chance of fooling the entire world by means of extortion. False promises and a long list of propaganda led this nonsense to create a solid ground by the means of mind control.

When someone takes the time to expose the concrete effects of mind control, that person will find himself or herself in wonder and fear of retaliation. When the truth is spoken, no matter from where or from whom, it should always provoke a reaction. Certainly, most sheep are too busy to read a book and search for information. Instead, they accept a load of brainwashing. This is the result of perfect and totalistic power governed by the mentor of evil-spirited individuals within the mind-control system.

In this chapter, I have exposed the positive and negative accomplishments of mind control upon hard workers, honest citizens, and vulnerable sheep, who have nothing to show for living every day with a lack of motives. For the one who takes pride upon himself or herself by confronting these monsters, he or she is soon sutured by mental pressure and physical abuse. These physical abuses take different forms. For example, at work, the proud will have to work harder for the same wage because there are simply too many sheep to feed. Companies feel the pressure of this liberal freeloader exploitation and are constantly searching how to minimize their costs because they also find themselves affected.

One other form of physical abuse comes from the free-loaders who are following in the footsteps of dependency by becoming egocentric and jealous of the one who puts pride into their life. The ones who choose to be proud citizens because of their will and hard labor become the constant targets of the sheep's jealousy. They are constantly criticizing conservatives because they are presumed to be the "rich" who need to pay more taxes because they possess more than the freeloaders.

This is where negative mind control has led society. Through the entire history of the world, puppeteers cannot stand resistance, for this resistance becomes a direct threat. Mind control somehow blinds the sheep to the point where the sheep agree with the agenda-controlled media and the puppeteers. For expected reasons, jealousy and envy are the fruits of such negligence on behalf of the freeloaders, and they are also a consequence of devilish mind control.

Mind control is a natural system to govern and regulate the source of life for every living species on Earth. Even animals are submit to a form of mind control, except they don't have the capacity we humans have. They follow their natural instincts that tell them what to do at any moment. Humans, however, are challenged by evil forces that constantly research how to control their minds. The evil forces are thirsty for power, money, and control, and nothing would make them come out of their dream of governing sheep affairs.

Mind control is also responsible for a lot of good deeds. A person with good intentions never fails to give a helping hand when he or she sees another in need. An individual's intention becomes the motive that activates him or her to help someone or to exploit someone. Choice has to play a great role in mind control because mind control by itself is death and serves nothing. Only an individual with a soul is able to direct his energy to use mind control, regardless if this individual has good intentions or bad ones.

Let us not be fooled by foxy string manipulators; they are sneakily introducing delusions under false promises of peace, happiness, fairness, equality, and above all, reward for others' hard work. The worst enemies of devilish mind control are the ones whose courage and perseverance become dominant through example and prosperity. We have to stay alert and scrutinize whoever is behind an offer when mind control is involved. Otherwise, we risk getting burned by his or her lies.

4

WHO ARE THE VULNERABLE?

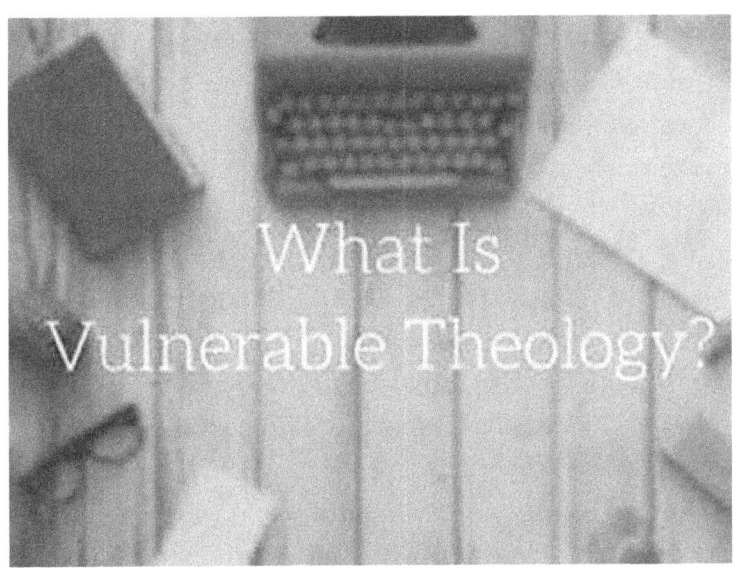

WE ARE ALL vulnerable to the immediate threat of mind control because exploitation can take many forms. Mind control has as much power as we individuals allow it to regulate and dictate our affairs.

The only way flowers will multiply is by being pollinated from the quiet work of bees visiting each flower for a brief moment. The contact between the bees and the flowers connotes marvelous teamwork. This is an excellent example of nature's controlled precision being silently accomplished every day. It also illustrates the positive trajectory of mind control. Flowers and bees are two species totally apart from one another, but they share what they have been programmed to do. The end result is the bee going to his beehive with the fruit of his work, while the flower is given the opportunity to reproduce.

I chose this example because it parallels our own way of functioning. The flowers and the bees play their role in nature and achieve what they have been programmed to achieve. We humans have been given ten times more functions than these species, so one hundred times more teamwork is needed in order to follow in the footsteps of what nature's example offers us.

I would like to share two little details I noticed about bees and flowers: the bee travels miles away from his home to search for pollen, and the flowers stand still and go nowhere. The bees have to expend an enormous amount of energy to travel every day to retrieve the pollen. The flower is stationary, standing in the middle of nowhere, exposed to every changing element.

The flowers are exposed to the law of hibernation during winter, and when spring comes, they are resurrected and reproduce leaves that are soon followed by a flower. In a sense, they die during cold weather and rejuvenate during warm weather. As for the bees, their work and travel paid off because they also hibernate during the winter, yet the difference is they have worked during the summer to create their own survival. Their survival food is what we call honey, and it is like the bees know they only have so much time to work in order to survive during cold weather.

The bees are straightforward with their duties because their survival depends on it; the flowers are negligent because they seem not to care about the future. The only moment that counts for the flower is the weather combination of rain and sunshine. As for the bees, they have to put in effort every day during summer to find the pollen and retrieve their food in colder weather.

Now let me compare this scenario to our society and the way we choose to live and build a foundation for the next generation.

Nature has so many lessons to teach us, but it cannot force us to learn because it is allowed to perform only up to a certain degree. This is where we connect directly with nature because we live among natural laws. As a matter of fact, nature is what allows us to survive. We see two categories of species performing in harmony, while the time is ripe for the bees and the flowers to give each other a helping hand.

In a society, we have three different kinds of personalities. The first is the one who takes care of his or her responsibilities and raises his or her family honestly. The second is the one who does not care about life, having lost all sense of pride and lives just like the flower, day in and day out. The third is the one whose actions resemble a fox's ruse, helping the "poor one" to establish and find a place in society.

The difference between nature and man-made ideologies is that nature follows natural boundaries, rules, and dictations. As for the fox in society, he or she creates his or her own ways and visions and then sneakily imposes his or her will upon vulnerable sheep looking for a free ride. All that these fox personalities demand in exchange for their service is the freedom of their sheep. It's not that the sheep are not free to do whatever they want, but they willingly submit to live in the boundaries of the fox's rules and regulations.

In a sense, sheep are deprived from their liberties without realizing it; they are totally at the mercy of these mercenaries. These foxy, "intelligent" individuals have succeeded in controlling the everyday activities of their sheep. But how do they succeed in their masterly plan of mind control? Well, they control how much their sheep receives on days when money is allowed in the signed contract. That contract clearly defines specific criteria for "the neediest sheep" who have to possess to receive what these foxiest of society have defined as sheep ways of life.

This chapter is not concluding that welfare programs are no good and should not be allowed. I do recognize that because nothing is perfect in nature, we have some individuals who have to seek help to survive. I also honor the patriot who gives his or her all to defend this beloved country, never backing down in the face of sacrifice to give the sheep opportunities to leech onto compassionate, helping hands.

It is very hard to expose an issue of this caliber, knowing it has the potential to be taken out of context. Most of the time, the people who are easily offended when the truth about ruling and poor choice hit are the sheep who have chosen this kind of life. The individual who takes pride in his or her life would read this without a problem. This is a good example of positive mind control versus negative mind control imposed onto honest citizens.

Vulnerability is not a sign of weakness. To acknowledge our vulnerability means we have given into another game plan. Actually, it is a sign of wisdom. To be able to recognize vulnerability creates a chain of events, and the one who is able to approach the subject without fear is not exposed to the negative effects of mind control. In most cases, where we find experience, we also discover struggles and failures. But these moments are not the ones that define individual personalities. What defines a personality is the determination that one individual chooses to adopt while confronting adversity.

For example, a little negligence on our behalf will cause us to trip and fall down because we did not tie up our shoelaces. Let's use this as an example of a little positive education in the mind-control field. This example stipulates that we are in control of our actions; everything depends upon our sense of responsibility to our own selves. Sometimes little details are the most precarious, and it is highly recommended that we imagine the big picture.

Mind control is a field of opportunities toward success and freedom as much as it is a field for creating chaotic losses. The ones who choose to be governed by the belief of having no choice accentuate a field of abuse and dictation. The ones who choose to stand up and fight the might of a regime that imposes vulnerabilities on behalf of the puppeteers, every day pulling their strings are far more ahead in life. This is where contrast takes form, and you start to see the fruit of such mind control and division among societies.

For the ones who choose to abide by false promises, they are never satisfied with their lives and always want more free items and offers. They feel the whole world owes them a living, and they truly believe they are victims of injustice when they look around and see others having success in life. Vulnerabilities take their true form and shape, and the fruit of dependency becomes the seed of jealousy. The same sheep, surrendering by choice, walk around in a field of dictation that governs their day-to-day activities because puppeteers now control their resources and revenue.

These individuals have no choice but to accept and to go along with mental and physical privation because this is the fruit following the tree of vulnerability in the mind-control field. Why do some individuals who do not realize their own destiny fall to jeopardy the day they choose to accept vulnerability as their mentor? The only logical answer in my view is that these individuals reflect the shadow of who they really are when they look in the mirror. The reflection of one object, depending on the angle and distance, could look different, but it is the same target. Nothing has changed while walking closer.

This brings me to say that life is a field of positive magnitudes and powers, but it could also be a negative field adopted by negligence and resulting in disastrous consequences. Each one of us is the chief of our own destiny, and no one can claim the other a success or a failure. These are the consequences each one of us chooses while making the right or wrong decisions in the personal affairs of our lives.

In this chapter, I referred to the needy who cannot provide for themselves. I also honored the soldiers who have given everything and all to defend their beloved country. I want to make sure these two categories of individuals are not confused with the freeloaders or the never-satisfied, envious individuals. This chapter about vulnerability is not about blaming, finger pointing, or denigration. It is about facts versus illusions and false promises.

One bad apple could very well be severed from the rest before it corrupts the whole apple tree. It only takes the will and the awareness to notice that there is a rotten apple. One responsible action from a vigilant individual could result in the safety of the whole crop of apples. The same scenario exists for a careless, negligent, vulnerable, and mind-controlled individual.

It is always easier to be negligent than to be a responsible individual. When an individual chooses to be negligent, he or she gets everything for free, but when an individual chooses to be responsible, he or she gets everything through dedication and pride. The two are enemies of each other because they are incompatible and cannot survive on the same tree. The strength of pride is the envy of the coward. The dire consequences we face every day while we pick and choose who we want to be remembered as.

Puppeteers who have spent many hours studying the field of mind control presented as a form of "vulnerability" are fully aware of the power they gain from their ideologies. These manipulators will be remembered as who they truly are: exploiters. It is always good to remember this fact of life: everything in this world finish to be exposing in the open. This divulging of secrets may take centuries or one day. At this point it makes no difference; once the actions are groomed and executed, the choice of the vulnerable individual becomes reality.

We cannot change history; we can only be a part of history. Our actions and vulnerable individuals are the foundation of the next generation. The telling of a fable and the telling of reality are identical because both are formulated by chosen words. The differences come at the end of the story, when the distinction is made between fiction and fact. When it comes time to face facts, we have no other choice but to adjust our knowledge.

The world possesses a choice to reproduce the fable or to stick to the facts while memorizing newly discovered events. It does not change the facts; they happened centuries ago. The same sentence is our legacy. No one will be able to change the shadow of history, but anyone can add and multiply upon fiction stories. Sheep, under the spell of vulnerability, usually love fiction because it gives them a special interest. Fiction corroborates the ideology of what the programmed mind wishes for: nothing but the fiction of "this is a wonderful life."

Vulnerability does not stand for excuse and reason, so why is it okay to give up on life as an easy way out of an individual's responsibilities? Vulnerability, however, leans toward laziness and extortion and making a living on behalf of the courageous. I repeat again that I am not talking about legitimate cases where it is obvious that caring help is needed. Also, I want to clarify one more time that this does not in any way target veterans, whom I admire for their sacrifice and willingness to confront dangerous situations.

However, there will always be some bad apples who will try to initiate the idea that I am against socialism because I am exposing the abuses of the system. Every time you touch a subject as sensitive as the one of mind control, there will be some lone wolf who will cry persecution. These potential individuals are most likely engaged in leeching off the system. It is not because you receive benefits under your right to receive them that exposing the truth becomes embarrassingly unbearable.

Frankly, I prefer that the programmed, low-class individuals consider me a bigot and a conservative mogul because I earn my living honestly with dignity and pride. Everyone is subject to the reality of mind control; however, not everyone is void of self-esteem. I believe in a helping hand, but it is a slippery slope because this helping hand opens the door to potential abuse and exploitation. On the behalf of a helping hand, the puppeteers who promote a free, socialist life achieve their goal for total control.

Exposing a dangerous situation has nothing to do with negligence of free will because it has nothing to do with the false promise of happiness. Compassion has nothing to do with extortion; however, compassion has everything to do with common sense. I know that this chapter might aggravate individuals who fall into the category of the puppeteer. Let me be clear: mind control is not a trial for exploitation or the source of study to find advantages. There will always be needy people, and there will also be criminals who, at first sight, will cheat, rob, provoke, confront, protest, and the list of abuse goes on.

There is only one reason for an independent individual to earn his life if he has the capacity: the love for independence. The one who chooses not to give in to the easy way out is the one who will pay that noble price. Those individuals will be the center of jealousy because their choice for freedom will support their quality of life. I have always liked the saying, "Where there is a will, there is a way." It is unfortunate when I witness so little interest from sheep to acquire independence.

These same sheep pass the majority of their time glued to the television, getting indoctrinated by a controlled media. I don't want to finish this chapter on a negative note, but honestly, I just can't resist. After all, it is all about what sheep do to make it happen. There is a time in life when we have to stop and think about our future and what we leave behind for future generations. Mind control has a role to play because nature is fulfilled by control; however, nature is not fulfilled by exploitation. We are the ones who create exploitation and negative mind control to the point where we are constantly working against ourselves.

The end of this chapter is hard to conclude because there is so much to talk about, as there are so many realities and painful situations to face with courage. The mental program of "What can I get for free?" doesn't guide everyone. Instead, there is a great quantity of individuals choosing to stand up for their principles. It only takes one too many ingredients to ruin the best meal and ruin a master chef's dreams. While this is the truth, the chef has two choices: cry over the fact that he failed or fix his mistake for a brighter tomorrow.

Experiences are our vital signs; if we weren't allowed to make experiences, we wouldn't have a chance to rectify what went wrong. Experience has a lot in common with determination and pride when positive motivations are found. Negative attitudes destroy the point when individuals will choose to adopt a new attitude after having failed in one of their projects.

5

WHO BENEFITS FROM MIND CONTROL?

W<small>E ARE UNDER</small> a shadowed umbrella with multiple anterior skeletons that had benefited from mind control at time had become real human turning into ghost when needed. Mind control is like a doorway into a home; once you have access, you are allowed to enter the home. Once you have entered the residence of a mind-controlled area, you have to be careful not to divulge the knowledge that you are mentally exposed. If, by negligence, you fail to keep your oath of secrecy and reveal the content of your findings, some consequences will soon knock on your door and become your reality.

You may never see it coming your way, and you may also see it approaching your way, depending on the judgment that the mind-control masters would have rendered on your behalf. For some, the danger the mind-control masters represent is too eminent. The quick solution to keep control over leaks of secrets is to end one's existence under inexplicable circumstances. Mind control falls under the control of a few chosen individuals who are given access to the might of the study made upon this natural, orderly need.

For some reason, even the elite who are permitted to interact directly with the consequences of mind control do not trust each other. There are systems put in place where strict resolution and demand are formulated. No one but the master sitting on his throne of mind control is allowed to use the field of mind control. Rest assured, no one really knows at that level who is the master. This chapter should not, by any means, be classified as a conspiracy theory, which some might believe this content falls under.

Really, who are the ones who directly benefit from a mind-controlled environment? This is a good question because the one who has asked might have received their answer. For some reason the answer never came to the surface for the general public, and why? How? These simple menaces inspire fear, followed by the threat of torture or scared to be made an example. These are four specific ways authors of mind control are using. The first one is author of mind control cherish to flash pure intentions, the second is they love to seed moments of uncertainty the third one is they advocate false pretenses the last one is they enjoy when target bow to master planning. Every day there are more techniques developed in order to keep the leads secure, but I am just talking about the general one.

These means are also being used outside of the domain of mind control to indoctrinate the general public who is unaware of being scammed by a few elites. There are five major sources where mind control benefits the leader: non-profit organizations, religious institutions, charity institutions, foundations, and also branches of government institutions.

In every situation, there are good and vital forces as much as there is devilish superiority tarnishing the positive side of the legitimate rights that nature offers us. Do not judge every one of these organizations; instead, take a critical look at these organizations. Sure, we have to pay close attention because these organizers like to use secrecy while they perform their duties. Confidentiality will always be a wonderful means to keep tabs on sensitive information to justify a movement.

For example, there are several levels in the domain of foundations. The only one who benefits from a "donation" is the one who contributes to the movement. The one who receives the donation has to ensure that the source receives acknowledgment for the gift. There is no such thing as a free ride when we fall into the domain of who benefits from mind control because everything is weighed and precisely calculated.

We have to maintain a fair balance while exploring the domain of what or who is behind an organization because appearance can sometimes be very tricky. Open minds are required every time we consider rendering a judgment upon someone or some organization's actions. If we have a closed mind at the start of analyzing a situation, we do not possess the ability to be impartially focused. We risk the danger of examining and following the case with a missed opportunity to really grab the depth of an investigation. Every element is important while we scrutinize the pros or cons of a situation where we legally have the right to suspect profit or hidden abuses.

The more you entrust someone to execute the will of his or her electoral power, the more this individual is given the power to tap into the phenomenon of mind control. There is a whole new universe that peels off, just like we peel an orange before consuming it. Freedom is a guaranteed right for every one of us who live on this planet; this is a natural right we are given at birth. This is why mind control plays an important role in the well-balanced system of nature, as everything operates and is coordinated by natural laws.

Now this does not become an automatic token for the elected one to build a wall of secrecy and do whatever he or she wants. Consequences follow every decision and action when this entrusted individual is given the power to fulfill his or her promises. Just like the citizen has to abide by the community's voting choices, the elected one has to abide by the will of the citizens. Of course, the momentary power only lasts for a couple of years, but the consequences last for a long time and are sometimes irreversible.

The justice system is based upon five factors: discoveries, facts, witnesses, testimonies, and franchises. These five factors are at the center of how the elected one will benefit from mind-control power. The power of mind control is by far the wonder of the ignorant and the assault of the one who studied how to penetrate this universe. Surprisingly, what often occurs is that most of us (if not all of us) cannot survive without some kind of control.

To be a beneficiary of knowledge in controlling others, one must consider himself or herself well above their mate. Another form of the benefits of mind control is religion. Not that religion is bad by itself, but what individuals choose to believe can be consequential. Not everyone is pure of heart and seeded with good intentions; there is some usurping done on the behalf of criminals. These criminals may have a public record of good deeds and examples, but most of the time, after a closer look, we discover they are not so good examples.

In the domain of faith versus religion, there are two distinctive outcomes: the first one is that no one can access faith, and the second one is that religion is the door to access faith. There is a perfect example of two domains pointing to the same horizon, surprisingly working hand in hand. The beneficiary of mind control is for each one of us, depending upon how much effort we put into this domain.

Some people would prefer to be good followers of laws and regulations, but they lack investigation and research into the domain of exploitation. For others, they will be skeptical about mind control, referring to it only as a conspiracy theory. Others will be infuriated and will revolt against mind control because they perceive the positive side of good manners and the devastating effects of exploitation. I am sure everyone is familiar with the term "establishment." I looked up the definition in the dictionary out of curiosity, and this is what it said: "The action of establishing something or being established, establishment of a scholarship, renews that personal interest of donors in students."

It is interesting that the following are synonyms of establishment: foundation, institution, formation, inception, and creation—all falling into the paved way of mind control. Even the dictionary confirms that mind control is the power to unlock all possibilities. Individuals must understand and study the criteria of the strength of mind control. Then these same individuals or groups of people have become vested with institutional authority within a society, especially those who control civil services and the government.

This is a serious business—nothing to be taken lightly—because of the consequences implied when those individuals assume their "responsibilities." The Establishment generally denotes a dominant group or elite class that holds power or authority in a nation or organization. The Establishment is most often a closed social group with specific, entrenched structures, either in government or within specific institutions. This is the new measure of power and control combined together that has been created for our generation.

Not only will our generation be affected by the pressure of the inadequate proportions of the power of mind control and the general public. The generation following domination will surely try to curb some of the bad effects of things that occurred prior to their existence. The problems among this future generation will be remnants. For example, once you have a taste of fame and power, you always want more. It becomes a drug that is difficult to satisfy.

The thirst for crooked extortion of power becomes hard to refute because of the benefits and powers hidden behind the magical means of mind control. Frankly, the beneficiaries of mind control are the ones who abandon their self-esteem, loyalty, and morality in exchange for temporary power and control. I am talking about negative situations where power diverges from loyalty, truth, and fairness, and where individual choices become someone's legacy. No one thinks about legacy because that day does not exist where one can witness his or her legacy.

If we were to consider our legacy, both personally and in the larger context of society, I believe there would be less abuse and exploitation among the elite's establishment systems. We would most likely be able to let other individuals weigh in with their opinions and observations. Of course, there is always a fine line in any field and circumstance—this is what we call wisdom. Wisdom and negative mind control are not so friendly with one another, although they could work together as a pair. However, wisdom is far more advance responsible to regulate positive mind control and destroy negative effects of mind control with logic.

Why is wisdom far more advanced than mind control? The answer for me is that wisdom arrives most of the time only after learning a costly lesson or witnessing a good and fruitful moment. Yet it is rare to encounter wisdom without experience—not that this is impossible, but we have a tendency to trust only ourselves. Sometimes wisdom is gained from books, education, and memory recall, but above all, wisdom is gained from our own experience. Life is all about a massive experiential moment given to us as a gift; it is up to each of us to honestly appreciate the gift or choose to exploit it.

For the most part, crooks use religion to gain the maximum amount of mind control. Having said this, it would be totally unfair to gather all religions in the same category. As always, there are bad apples here and there, ruining the reputations of honest preachers. We have a need for a good moral compass in society and for religion to create an atmosphere of fairness and honesty. It is odd for me to write this, as my next sentence introduces the idea that religion is a synonym for exploitation. However, faith and religion are two different things.

Religion is a man-made creation that tries to put in perspective the tangibility of faith. Faith has survived centuries of adversity, and religions have found their nourishment in the faith of the people. Faith is the source of good deeds and compassionate change throughout the universe. However, religion is used as a means to extort goods by preaching the "truth" to gain money, power, and control.

Two universes gather in one cycle, where basically anyone with a little education can find a way to gain their living without having to work hard. It is a slippery trade because while religion is exploiting the good name of faith, these man-made religions are not immune from scandal. It is a misfortune that we encounter mind control, dictations, and persuasions among those "teaching of the purest truth that comes along with religion." It is our duty to constantly investigate and to scrutinize activities where exploitation and extortion are a possibility.

Those duties fit elected public servants as much as any members of different categories of ecclesiastic hierarchy. Let us look at the definition of religion, according to the dictionary: "Religion is a set of beliefs concerning the cause, nature, and purpose of the universe, especially when considering as the creation of superhuman agency. It usually involves devotional and ritual observances, and often contains a moral code governing the conduct of human affairs."

This form of duty is to be traced where a specific, fundamental set of beliefs and practices exist and is generally agreed upon by a number of people or a world council of religions. The practice of religious beliefs and ritual observance of faith is something individuals choose to believe. Preachers using religion for personal gain often use an exalted tone to persuade his or her faithful to devotedly follow his or her teaching. These puppeteers announce the "good news" angle as a matter of ethics, and of course conscience, in order to make religion reflect their fight against prejudice.

In this chapter, I point out the danger and potential abuses we encounter anywhere we have opportunists. These individuals make honest and sincere individuals who are not religious look as if their choices are immoral. It is unfortunate that even religion becomes a target for exploitation, extortion, reeducation, coercion, and even thought control and/or reform. This is one of the big pictures behind the wall of secrecy that controls how we dress, speak, and interact with each other and members of the church.

The sooner we use our given senses, the sooner we will create an atmosphere where opportunists would not be able to survive. Unfortunately, the grass is always greener outside of the fence, and the temptation to acquire this grass has become a must, while most of us fall for the false promise of greener grass. This "divine nourishment" is an opportunity that will eventually render opportunist's rich and render followers into poor slaves.

I am in no way suggesting that religion is the base and the cause of every bad situation—far from it. I am simply exposing the danger of blind religion versus true faith. While I am exposing the danger of exploitation in religion, I am made to step back into my own belief system. All I can say is how vulnerable we are when the time comes when adversities serving us more than what appear for a brief moment fair share. Most of the time, when we turn toward religion, it is for relief in moments of doubt, confusion, anxiety, deception, and, above all, in times of deep distress.

This is the perfect ground for opportunists to offer counsel, sympathize, send good wishes, or to plant the seed of "good news" from the Bible, or whatever other material religions offer. Nevertheless, when we face moments of fragility, the door is open for exploitation through compassionate means. I will not end this chapter bashing the negative side of religion, but I want to encourage everyone to be responsible. Not everyone is out to get us or to take advantage of a situation gone haywire; this is why wisdom is acquired and not freely given.

Experience is the healing of many situations gone wrong because now we possess the knowledge to avoid what once made us vulnerable. If we were to enlist all the experiences we have had during our lifetimes, we would be surprised to see an inevitable personal growth. Sometimes wisdom comes to us not the way we really want, but when we are forced to adapt to the consequences of our actions.

Beware of your surroundings in the vast universe of exploitation. If you don't, sooner or later, you will fall victim to attack from opportunists. This concludes the chapter about "who benefits from mind control." My hope is that my readers will find something to influence their choices in their life and experiences.

6

WHAT ARE THE CONSEQUENCES?

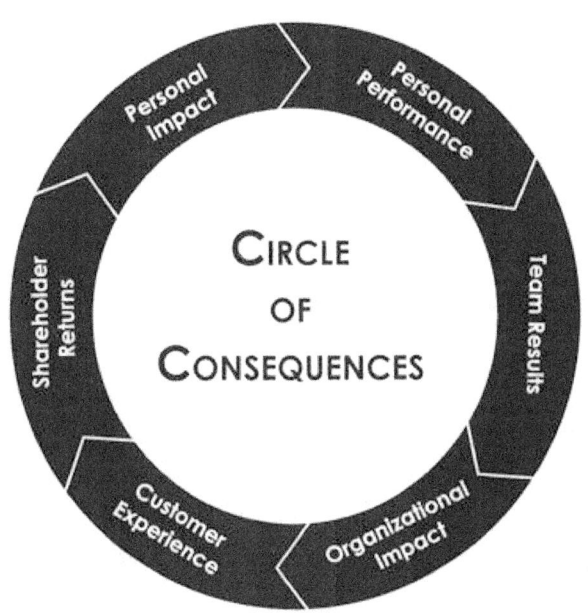

THIS IS A question at times that is very hard to answer. However, it appears in multiple circumstances and is really easy to find the answer to. What are the consequences of mind power? This simple question opens a horizon of doubts, wonder, catastrophic events, surprises, and deceptions. The main topic of this chapter elaborates on what effects of mind power are possessed by each individual forming a society.

For many, the experience of mind power will be a joyful remembrance of the expertise that the powerful had provided to them. There will also be opportunists who would testify how much mind power had enabled them to get powerful and known in society. There are also those who desperately cry for justice because their lives have been shredded by the cruelty of mind power.

Mind control is found in many environments. It will most likely be more noticeable in families, in religious creeds, and in specific cases with individuals who are considered bullies. There are multiples faces when we approach the subject of the direct and indirect consequences of mind control. Depending on the individual, mind control is revealed in motives and goals, and he or she is often unaware of his or her effect on others in his or her blind consummation of power and domination.

The consequences of well-managed mind control are the pride of societies, the continuation of good moral behavior, the fruit of good deeds over multiple generations, and, above all, respect and longevity of wisdom. Wisdom is a wonderful quality that stands out from all other unnecessary words. This simple word lays the path to the flourishing and prosperity of all nations because wisdom is a quality that requires a natural disposition to acquire.

In order to have the will and the disposition to obtain wisdom, we have to envision all the possibilities occurring when we dispense ourselves in any way. It requires the individual seeking wisdom to scrutinize and educate himself or herself about the positive side of mind control. If we had paid a little more attention to the benefits of positive interactions with wisdom, we would make such progress as a universe in little or no time at all. We would find unity and teamwork, which would enable this discovery to be bestowed upon future generations.

Not everything is a source for negativity; there are multiple sources of good deeds and examples transpiring from sources of good mind control. We need to educate ourselves not only through media sources but also through efforts to read and research our own history, which is the history of the world we live in and how previous generations influenced our own generation and family values.

Wisdom becomes the only choice of individuals who demand respect and are constantly researching how to acquire a higher quality of life. We are given opportunities every day to interact with wisdom, and no one can change someone else's attitude or disposition. The consequences for individuals who have chosen lasting wisdom are prosperity, remembrance, and legacy. There is nothing glorious in being remembered as a good sheep, as a follower, as simple minded. What is glorious is the character of individuals who are not afraid to stand up to insanity, lies, and deception.

Wisdom gives us an occasion to scrutinize, educate, discover, and sort out the lies and truths, although more lies will be uncovered than truth. This is the consequence of knowledge versus fables. Wisdom is for everyone interested in being exposed to the ray of wisdom. Why does there seem to be just a small portion of our humanity devoted to graciously expose the benefits of wisdom? That question is easily answered if you ask on a daily basis, living and believing as most citizens.

In order to be exposed to the field of natural wisdom, we have to want to be illuminated by the shining light of knowledge. Wisdom is the fruit of determined dispositions that experiment with a life that is guided with knowledge and prudence. These two qualities become a vital part of the individual while he or she exposes himself or herself to the ray of wisdom. I will add a personal note: prudence is always granted when individuals ask a question and expect an answer.

The source telling the lies may not like these individuals who use knowledge, and they will be subject to discrepancies and vicious attacks upon their person and beliefs. They may very well be made an example of "homegrown terrorism" and some will disappear under pretenses of suicides, overdoses, or mysterious and inexplicable circumstances. History will attest to the fact that when one uses wisdom to investigate a situation, he or she is silenced, again under mysterious circumstances.

The inner ring of elite puppeteers pulling the strings do not like when individuals stand up for their rights and freedom because these avenues pave the way to wisdom. The more you interrogate and question what the news media are reporting, the more you are considered to be an outsider. To me, it becomes an honor to be considered an outsider if I possess the power of knowledge given to me by my search for wisdom.

This chapter has so far explicated the positive side of the consequences of mind control. By doing so, I am sure the reader will be able to see that even if my book has an abundance of negatives, I try to counterbalance with the positives. Mind control has the potential to enrich good and loyal behaviors as much as it has the potential to demonize the result of positive actions done by evil mind control.

Everything depends upon the disposition of individuals to collaborate and work hand in hand with wisdom or to choose to neglect such precious gifts. When individuals refuse wisdom, they put their future at risk. Life is a perpetual field of choices, and at the end of the day, these choices will be where we lay that night. Nothing will be able to change the outcome of our pride and integrity or the deception of cowards and indifference.

We, alone, will have to enter our created legacy that we have already been classified by or with the help of the individuals who possess wisdom. Why are there so many haters? For me, the answer is simple: not enough individuals stop and think with their heart. Why are there multitudes of faiths and beliefs working directly against each other? Then again, the thirst for total power is exemplified in the consequences of destruction, serving as an example of surrendering the sheep who may have doubt about the creed and faithfulness of their leaders.

There are some circumstances that are mistakenly misjudged but also on purpose through the media sources to trick the ones who do not take seriously their reason for seeking wisdom. For example, a hate crime committed under the pressure of leaders in the name of religion becomes classified as lunatic, bipolar, or the actions of a lone wolf and racist. The real truth is never spoken, and if it comes to the surface, it is camouflaged and made almost impossible to sort out the illusions and the facts.

Only wisdom is able to unveil a little corner of the scenario well-guarded by the cautious puppeteers pulling their hidden strings. Sometimes the truth about "new developments" are so overwhelming and disturbing that it is hard to believe that humanity could descend so low. When you do not allow wisdom to participate in your personal life, you leave the door wide open for a cesspool of nonsense to overshadow your own existence and knowledge.

I am sure if the radio and the media would spend more time exposing the benefits of wisdom, we would be far more advanced in technology and understanding. This is unfortunate, in a sense, because we would be wasting our precious time waiting for this to become reality. Everything depends upon choice, adherence, creed, teaching, example, and pride.

Now I will step into the negative effects of mind control that can become a disaster. Today, there are many tactics deployed to regulate, control, and rewrite the laws of common sense. We find ourselves much more involved in a provocative, man-made ideology, leading to perfect chaos presented as unity and an acceptable society.

The first step of negative mind control by persuasion is to impose limits on the mental development of an individual's personality. This is not a small task, yet up to now, mind control seems to not have fully succeeded in this project. There are of course masses of populations who freely choose to be guided by their nose to safety under false promises. These individuals are the ones who pave the way to complete chaos and disaster. Once these individuals surrender, the door to prejudice is open.

The one who controls the sheep enjoys a momentary victory with a foundation made of restriction, subsistence, disposition, and, above all, exploitation. Nothing adheres as well as false promises, eloquent speech, bribery, ambiguity, and pretention. The preferable opening phrase in a speech of self-defense by the one who set up a field of mind control is, "I did not have…" or "I don't remember breaking any laws…" or "Everything I did was approved…"

Their stance has already been set up to come to their defense, even though sometimes they get cornered by lies that are covering other lies. They have a tendency to abide by and rule under the same excuses that exploitation disguises and deceptive manipulations. Nothing is more consistent in the mind of a sick control freak than repeating examples, times, places, and consequences. This barrage of false instructions and deception amazingly has rapid progress in the unconscious mind of the sheep. Having already bowed to the pressure of negligence in ruling their own affairs, these sheep arrive to inexistence if deprived of the lies coming from their mentors. Once this step is established, the product of negative mind power is fully marching toward total control over an empire of delusions, lies, and deceptions.

The second step involves persuading the sheep to depend upon delivering the wonders that the master of mind control arrives at. This second step will control the sheep's thoughts and their individual mechanisms. Now the population of sheep will arrive at a nonexistent stance if the puppeteers tell them this is not allowed or it is deadly. They submit right away without examining why this is not allowed or why this is considered a mortal situation.

Under false pretenses, puppeteers are free to roll in their agenda and their library of news and explanation of further development occurring around the world of sheep. Unaware and predisposed individuals once at the level of conscience will swallow all information transmitted. It many cases it won't make a difference if the "new development" can be retraced by investigation; what counts is the potency of good phrasing. Nothing works better than using the actual moment of war and revolt to help the solidification of independence.

Having said this, it is important not to categorize all sources of media as mind-controlled agitators and programmers. The awareness created by wisdom will ensure the ones who are not sheep will not disregard potential information given through a medium of lies. Nothing works better to cover up an agenda than confusing individuals with stories mixing ten lies with one truth. This small portion of the truth is a vital game charger for the puppeteers, whose goal is to deceive by prank, audacity, and exploitation.

The trust and belief in the news media becomes an active field where intelligence can sometimes be overshadowed by audacity and believable lies. This illusion comes thanks to the brilliance of deception, which uses reality to transform a report into a pit of ambiguity and wonder. Most of the time, the puppeteers' big picture does not even reflect the truth about the story reported on the news channel. Deception will cover up all evidence of fraud by enhancing and pushing the field of personal reflection.

They will finish their presentation with a quote from the presumed hateful individual to push their agenda for control and cover up any signs that their story is nothing but a fraud. The lives of individuals do not matter anymore— only the substance counts that works to indoctrinate sheep. Public reports of investigation of the home or apartment of the target are widely televised to expose multiple eyes and comprehension.

At this point, mind control has made progress through the work of manipulation and control to deflect from the "maybes" or "I wonder," questions that individuals have a legitimate right to ask. The most crucial thing in this scenario is that once the news is delivered, no one is able to reach the point of the diffusion within the story reported. There may be a chance to let to sheep give their thoughts about the developing tragedy. Very few have the opportunity to directly question the mastermind behind the chaotic event that has been reported and televised.

The reporter in charge of reporting the news to the general public often doesn't know his superiors, who have been instructed to publicly express the will of behind-the-scene puppeteers. So far very few have had the chance to verbally challenge these monstrous haters and bloodthirsty criminals with mind-sets of total and absolute power. Persuasion becomes the daily bread of rumors and deracination of the truth veiled by ambiguities in an agenda of covering up.

Today, there are lots of demands for "new regulations," stating that the dignity and rights of the individual fit within the domain of persuasion. It appears the media and their sources have won their masterly war against common sense and wisdom. Who benefits from these reports of chaos and haters sustained by creed, religion, and oath to an organization, or judged to be a lone wolf and bipolar? How long will this continue until the sheep wake up? Just wondering and compiling evidence to back up a cover up is enough to engulf and surrender without need for force whole society?

This is the fruit of negligence and indifferent attitudes that provide individuals with what they need and want. In return, they will forever endorse all the organization's materials. They will never question whose interest is at stake. Bribery and exploitation of the unconscious minds of sheep have resulted in their total dependency, and they have signed off on their liberty and right to choose to investigate and ask questions. This phase opens the door into thought reform, solidifying a mechanist ideology of turning what used to be legitimate into now forbidden and what used to be harmful into now lawful.

There is a lot at play in the domain of "What are the consequences of negative mind control?" Relying upon sheep and programmed individuals is the only way this agenda will succeed. Robots are a human innovation that has succeeded in rendering humans at the level of robots. Unlike the man-made robots, humans possess feelings, understanding, compassion, dignity, and pride. All these legitimate rights become the worst nightmare of society.

When these noble factors enriching our universe have been pushed toward one ideology and creed, they become the source of direct exploitation and demolition of a sound society. It is unfortunate we are witnessing the demolition of a whole generation at the hands of mind control and fraud, as well as witnessing their devastating consequences.

7

MIND CONTROL-FIT SOCIETIES

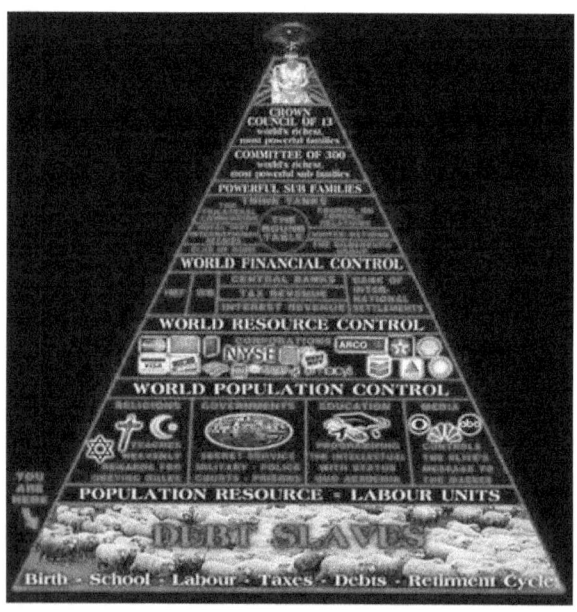

REGULATION AND CONTROL in nature is dominant, considering orderly nature constantly submits to harmony through the means of natural balance described with perfection the positive wonder of mind control. We have already looked into the need of mind control in nature; now let's take this to a new level where the wisdom of the Creator is alive in the quiet, natural, calm atmosphere provided. From the day, we are given the experience to know the wonder of nature, we are also submitting to nature and laws regarding nature.

Mind control–fit societies exist in harmony with natural laws and regulations dictated to us by our Creator, who does not impose its will upon any of us. When we find that the habitat of our planet is connected to an environment where dignity and naturally born rights are not tampered with, we are in a good atmosphere of mind control. Communion and substance are two elements we find when we adhere to pure intentions in accordance with the principles and wonder of good mind control.

Societies are destined to self-destruct if regulations and harmony are oppressed. Of course, we do not have the power to change this simple fact of life, although we are given the freedom to choose and pick our own avenues. Take laws and regulations out of circulation, and tragedy and self-imposed misery will soon bombard us if we do not accept the natural terms and laws of nature.

I am not trying to turn anyone against a system we call the "news media"; I am simply trying to create a link between mind control versus realities and facts. Sure, there are lots of true stories being reported on the news media system, but it seems to me that truth sometimes works with the expected results of a well-hidden provocation.

I also do not want anyone to think I am against any form of reporting and visual presentations of the scene gone wrong. All I am saying is that we are exposed to multiple factors and reasons that are sometimes not reported to create open fields to factors and realities often underestimated. Before casting judgment, we should always wait for further developments to see if anything comes out after the news media have done their work to talk about a specific situation. Wisdom requires allowing a moment of reflection for open minds to look at the whole picture, not just the report we are fed by the news media.

News media are in fact a good instrument to develop wonder in society; it fits well in the domain of the question "Are there mind control–fit societies?" Yes, every tool given to us is a wonder of natural knowledge developed over time by intelligences for the purpose of promoting other wonders. When we allow ourselves to rush to judgment to either condemn or to acquit an accused individual, we are acting like fools ruled by first impressions and maybe even ulterior motives.

Mind control does have a well-designed place, even in nature; everything we see and do has its place and order, properly designed, depending on our needs. We have to stop playing the ostrich game, hoping no one will notice mind control when danger becomes imminent. Nature is a good example because we are made to cohabitate with nature, sharing its beauty and goodness. However, what has not been noticed in nature is hypocrisy or a one-sided situation where ambiguities could be planted.

This is what I call intelligence because nature follows its designed role and given place. We humans are above all other creatures, as we are our own authors of prosperity or self-destruction. These two opposite qualifications are not imposed upon us by any way in nature. It is bestowed upon us by our own means, ideologies, perceptions, dedications, and above all, our choice to have a proud or indifferent attitude.

We cannot control the way nature has been dictated to procreate. However, we control the substance of advantages nature offers us. Choice is the mother of wisdom. If we weren't given an opportunity to render decisions, we would be just like nature submitting to a regime. We are not a regime, and since free choices control the environment, we are given the freedom to render wise and prudent decisions. Nature will not, under any circumstances, give us an example of distortion, false reporting, or justification to rush to judgment.

Only one source can achieve this, with the help of wisdom and freedom, and that is the human race, which lives among other living creatures in harmony. War and desolation will occur because of evil and partial reports and also because of those thirsting for power, dominance, control, and total indoctrination. It is a harsh truth to discuss when we have to confront the dangers of negligence, exploitation, and collusion.

If we did have any form of law and regulation expected from the living generation, we would be in situations that are a free for all. Orderly and justified mind control in our society creates balance and respect for the established laws and regulations. It gives us an opportunity to feel pride. Everyone knows a red light means stopping for a brief moment to share the road with another. What are the consequences of infringing upon these laws? A well-deserved ticket or an expected restitution, depending on the degree of transgression.

Another example of positive mind control in society is the expectation that citizens will drive sober. What is the consequence if we do not obey this positive mind-controlled idea? Under the influence of alcohol, our abilities to think and react are gravely affected when we get behind the wheel of a car. What are the consequences of this breaching of the law? If the offense results in involuntary murder, one will most likely be served with a life sentence in prison. For other cases, depending upon the gravity and the repetition of the same transgression, the death penalty could be recommended.

The family suffering from their loss will be in the courtroom, ecstatic to see justice prevailing upon a criminal who did not care about respecting a valuable mind-control situation. It is important to realize that any actions we impose are subject to other criticisms and observances. The only thing we are in control of is our actions, and the consequences fall onto the domain of evaluation from another sources exterior to us. We don't have the power to control other witnesses and their understanding, although we are fully in charge of our own choices and every little consequence as a result of them.

We are not and never will be the epicenter of the universe, although we are unique individuals who form and represent this vast universe. Taking this into consideration would create positive mind control in our society, which would, in turn, flourish with prosperity and wondrous legacies. The reason why we are not the epicenter of this planet is simple: this planet is only a passage. No one knows how long we will live in this habitat or what the future holds for generations to come after our passing.

We are members of this universe, but we are not the only masters. We only have control over our actions. This balanced control is totally in hand with the disposition to follow the natural guide that this universe has bestowed. We are, like it or not, subject to the Creator's natural, universal laws.

Our laws are based upon these unbreakable and immutable natural foundations, serving the base, constitutions, and guidelines to maneuver our own affairs. Mind control–fit societies can occur as long as this natural innovation is in perfect harmony with the dictations and expectations of the Creator. The Creator expects us living creatures to follow the basic institutions of all living things here on Earth because we are all under the same umbrella. There are many levels and responsibilities for perfect harmony to lead the way. The more freedom is allowed to exist, the greater the expectations, especially when we consider the phenomena of this gift called free choice.

We humans are the only ones in the whole Creation system provided with this marvelous privilege to engage in our own harmony and abide by natural laws or rebel against them. If, by choice, we agree to blindly follow the bad influence of mind control, we are vowed to self-destruct.

I will now step into the negative effects of the kind of mind control unfit to rule societies because of exploitation, dictatorship, and abuse of power. As always there will be a tragic split from the benefits of good, legitimate, and natural mind control. This control is only achievable because human knowledge wants to destroy what is legitimate to acquire prestige and perfect control.

Ideologies of control are a domain of mental manipulation using physical experiences. These two avenues are the same if we consider the soul as the motor of the body of an individual. The more puppet-controlling elites achieve to deepen their knowledge about negative control in society, the more their work of exploitation is ensured to rule and survive. It makes no difference if one of the puppeteers died; their legacy is already well planted and their replacement already groomed.

In some cases, there is a misunderstanding among the elite and then the media will report that this one or that one is deceased under mysterious circumstances. This secret universe of a caucus of evil should never be revealed if reveled severe action follows. The one judge guilty of revealing his or her knowledge is dealt with without mercy. I bet since World War II, half of the mysterious dead are directly connected with the power of knowledge.

Negative mind control has no place in a healthy society where honesty and teamwork are prime qualities. When honesty and teamwork exist, one feels noticeable inner peace. Just like natural laws are impervious to the effects of devilish mind control, society is a poison that eventually ends in war and revolt. For justification to provocation the rights of individuals are invoked and liberties are most likely the reason claimed to justify rebellion. Bad management among societies educated is bonded to gain ground in a terrorist's agenda.

While societies are vulnerable when submitted to natural, good mind control, there will always be some exploitation coming from opportunists. These individuals are not afraid to devour the remaining good that mind control has offered to the general public. They are not so obviously agile; they know how to present an agenda. They first look at the innocent to implement their mind control and then reveal themselves as destructive. This is the reason why we are facing so much disagreement among the elite; they do not particularly agree with the mode and desire of their colleagues.

The word "terrorist" was slowly imposed onto societies because over the years, the secret agenda of these opportunists shifted. Why have some of these secret agendas shifted? We are not immortal, and what was good for the prior innovators of control is not necessarily the best approach for the others. With a little knowledge, common sense, and analysis, we can surely observe the upward trend of terrorist actions.

This is the product of negative mind control upon a society. Negativity always results in problematic and discordant situations. In a mind-control situation, there is no need to convince sheep because they have already submitted to the ideologies of masters outside their own individualism. The planting of ideologies and sources to cast out crime comes from puppeteers secretly pulling strings.

With a population of sheep, who needs good soldiers? The answer to that is the outsiders who have to constantly be on guard using defense mode. But why? The answer is simple: these puppeteers have to constantly ensure that their kingdom does not come under attack due to wisdom. This is a wonder of nature and also of society—to possess some individuals who have the knowledge of wisdom to counterfeit a trance for total global control. The number of wise individuals is, in my view, fewer than the ones whose goals are to enslave the whole universe under their dictations.

There are many reasons for the decline of wisdom. Here a few of them, though I am sure my readers will be able to come up with their own lists:

- Most individuals do not take time to read because it demands effort.
- Sheep let well-calculated promotional momentum distract them.
- It is easier to turn on the television or the radio and listen to the puppeteers' secret agenda.
- An indifferent attitude occurs when one is deprived of his or her negligent lifestyle.
- Accepting a prejudicial agenda promoted on behalf of the puppeteers is subject to anything that makes sense and creates positive avenues.
- Above all, facing the push of these mind control monsters is to prescribe to the notion of conspiracy theory.

Of course, anyone and everyone who opposes the agenda of secret puppeteers is dying for control and considered to be in immediate danger by the inner corps of elites. Wisdom is the power of almighty nature and is above all human laws because nature's laws are immutable. In one strike, nature could forever destroy the plan of elites. Pretention leads to audacity, rendering individuals blind when they believe they are invincible.

Until the day we face the reality that we are a community created to share ideas and talents received at birth, we will be harvesting our own glory with our miseries and anguish. Also, the day we stop competing with each other for power, control, and money will be the day we are instructed by the knowledge of wisdom. Until then, we set a sad vision and example for the next generation. Mind control is a complicated field of experience, learning, and discovering, and it is hard to manage if not guided through wisdom.

Today, more and more human error causes disaster, and the demolition of our society seems to be imminent. Small groups of pretentious individuals driven by their wealth pretend to be the lords and sovereigns of Earth. In their audacity, they forget where they come from and what their real destiny will be. We are all made to educate ourselves, depending on our choices, good or evil. There is no other way around it. I guess death is only good for the neighbor until the day comes and knocks on our own door. By then, the result of individual efforts and work will never be rewritten, and nothing will change our own individual legacies. Bad management, exploitation, and extortion will be forever sealed in the book of destiny and reflected on by future generations. Wisdom requires a moment of silence in order to reflect while considering one project. If we do not provide this moment, it will be provided to us after our passing away.

When this time comes, we will be in direct contact with respect to our choices to have adhered to or to have disregarded interactions with wisdom. If we have chosen to make wisdom ours, we will be forever remembered as the result of positive mind control. However, if we have chosen to let our adversaries take control of our affairs, we will be remembered as dissolvers and destroyers of society. At the end of this chapter, my hope is that everyone who reads this brief exposé will stop and think with their heart. If after consideration, some discoveries need to be adjusted, we will take charge to correct our guiding-compass motives.

Together we are strong and can accomplish so much more than disasters, and the choice is ours. At the end of the day, let's all use our given talents and abilities to construct positive avenues that will lead to honorable legacies for future generations. If not, we will have to endure the negative consequences of our bigotry and thirst for complete power and control. By the way, we will never be able to achieve that goal, and we have to face this reality. Be man and woman enough to admit that we are vulnerable. Pretension will not lead us anywhere but to chaos and disorder.

8

CHILDREN AND MIND CONTROL

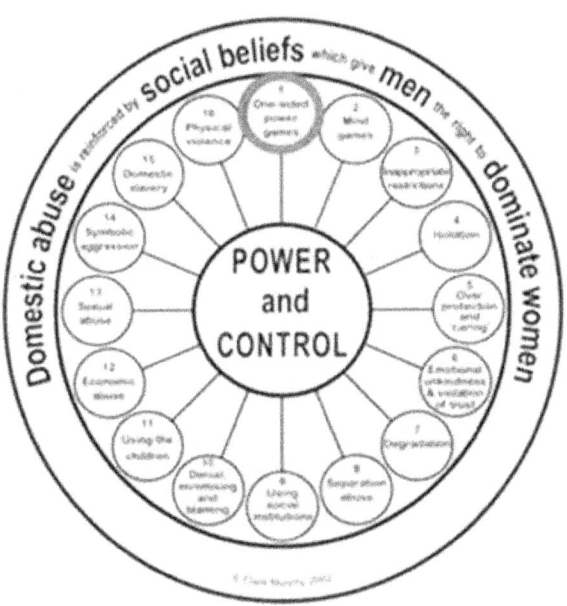

IN THIS CHAPTER, I will be focusing on education and the differences between a good education and a bad education—one that results in disaster. Our universal system is based on knowledge, invention, perception, imagination, creation, balance, regulation, and administration. These eight systems, among others, are the principles of knowledge versus examples of pure knowledge. When we were embryos, all these possibilities had been granted to us, and it took more than just one day to arrive where we are.

There are two forms of education that we encounter in our education system, with two different results. The first form of education would be exemplary, where family bonds and love prevail against any hardships. The second form of education would be indifference (i.e., "I really didn't want this kid, so let him do whatever he wants."). These two kinds of education become the foundation of our society like everything in perfect harmony when it comes to the complexities of our planetary system.

Once again, I will navigate the difference between examples of positive and negative education versus an education where no solid foundation is needed. There will be sharp contrasts between these two avenues. Nevertheless, they are the fruit of individuals given opportunities to choose to be responsible or to be negligent. The results in both cases are totally opposite to each other due to the great innovation of "free choice"; one will lead to success and the other to total disaster. I will now give special attention to the negative effects of an irresponsible attitude while children retrieve knowledge through education.

Knowledge is shared with the daily education we provide our future generations in order to operate and acquire their autonomy. Negative mind control has a specific role in the tragedies many children encounter while in the domain of education. Puppeteers use some children to initiate their style of learning, regardless if the child is being exposed to danger. Some other children choose to grab what looks to be the easy way out in developing their understanding of life in general. Others are careless about what they willingly expose their person to, dangers such as drugs, alcohol, cigarettes, porn, and the list goes on.

In the last category I mentioned, we encounter these children in a home where disorder is the norm, and order is something they might never have a chance to experience. In this category, the parents are at fault because they choose not to intervene. In most cases, they too are addicted to drugs, sex, and alcohol. Most of the time, adults don't have a clue that they will harvest what has been planted in their early age.

This is done with many deceitful tactics—bad examples, insane relationships, poor management, and neglected children. In this perfect environment of negativity, the destruction of not only the children but of a whole generation is possible. These traumas are so severe because these children have been rejected by the education that was taught to them.

For those unfortunate, unwanted children, bad mind control becomes their daily bread where they find substance for their survival. The most devastating situations when children become vulnerable occur when these children are exposed to child trafficking, child prostitution, and in some situations, child sacrifices to another "god." Perverted adults administer these devastations only to satisfy their own fantasies. These children in their early stages have their dignity as humans taken away from them; they live in deep depression and are disgusted with life in general.

Their little hearts endure what the adults have done to them, while they go to the street because they have nowhere to go. There are also runaway situations where dysfunctional parents have provoked their children to leave their family home. Another scenario comes from families who appear to be prosperous role models, but what no one else sees and hears behind closed doors is the demand for total control over the children's morality based upon previous traditions.

Why do I talk about these specific horrors in the education chapter? The answer is simple: tomorrow will be the day for the next generation to come forward and give testimony about the day before. When made a part of children's education, bad mind control plants concrete examples that lead the way to disorderly conduct, which increases the appetite of perverted individuals whose only desire is to exploit and hurt children. I mentioned sex exploitation of unwanted children running the street; there are other problems, such as addiction and drug abuse under the supervision of criminals.

We also find cases where religion is directly involved with these atrocities, and coming from that angle of abuse, children fall into despair. Religions come alive when some of us gather together in churches to worship, but abuse is not part of religion. It falls into the domain of "individual free choices." There will always be opportunists who will take my statement as wrong, but it does not change the fact that an institution should be incapable of perpetrating crimes upon children.

The notion of projecting the real guilt and monstrous actions through the medium of religious appearance is sometimes misleading. The problem is that the criminal, no matter the denomination, always finds a way to associate his or her mental sickness with the general appearance of an institution. Why is the appearance of a church or community relevant? Because from the beginning to the end, scandals have to be kept secret. Rest assured, nothing works better than a religious cover up.

Clerics in all forms of religion add their own guilt to the situation of what we call a "system of education," enabling us to underestimate the real root of the problem. "Why are we underestimating a portion of the root of the problem?" one may ask. The answer is "propaganda"—nothing works better to create a safe zone for criminals than to transform legitimate good to dangerous evil. This is without speaking about faulty branches in what we call an "elected public servant" who, in his or her own best interests, chooses to look the other way.

Is there some conflict of interest? Any time there is a smell of a cover up, there is evidence of potentially regrettable acts. Sometimes the perpetrators never see their day with justice on this Earth, and others, because of words, finally come under scrutiny. I don't want to spend the rest of this chapter talking about the negative consequences of bad education through the medium of mind control upon children. There is a lot more to be added to my little exposé, and I hope it will create a wake-up call for someone else to more deeply expose and write about these unacceptable abuses of children.

Now let us take a look at the positive avenues and wonder of natural law concerning children and mind control. Education is defined as "a wealth of knowledge acquired by an individual after studying particular subject matters or experiencing life lessons that provide an understanding of something. Education requires instruction of some sort from an individual or composed literature. The most common forms of education result from years of schooling that incorporates studies of a variety of subjects."

Now let us take a look at the definition of indoctrination. There are many interpretations offered in the dictionary. I chose one that, in my view, represents the description I believe is the best match for my topic. Indoctrination is served "to instruct in a body of doctrine or principles. Teach (a person or group) to accept a set of beliefs, uncritically broadcasting a vehicle for indoctrinating the masses, to instruct in a doctrine, principle, ideology, with a specific partisan or biased belief or point of view. It is also used to teach or inculcate to imbue with learning."

Let us now focus on the wonders of positive education. I have consulted the dictionary to discover the true meaning of the word education. Positive education promotes good behavior by following examples and experiences that we observe in one another. These observations are available to children whose parents assume their full responsibility. It also comes from honest teachers and friends, but the best teacher is one of parental love and dedication that reinforces positive education.

While a student receives knowledge about a specific subject at school, it is important to stay focused on whether he is retrieving the depth of positive exchanges that the child relies upon. Children also have a vivid sense of capturing their vision as a good example of a positive behavior. Observation and education work as a pair, competing with each other on a daily basis. For example, the way in which the parent relates to the child will impact their time in school.

Education is not only acquired by sitting behind a school desk, looking at a blackboard that details and describes instruction; it is also a commune of various little details. These little moments of truth are daily vessels that children navigate during their youth and into adulthood. We have to acknowledge the importance of a good example in contributing to the knowledge our children retrieve while at school. Education without example is a waste of time. At the end of the day, if what has been taught is not respected by others, then it is worthless. For parents, it is a good thing to remember their own time sitting at the school desk and learning what knowledge could be doing for them.

It is also a wise decision for parents to remember how vulnerable they were as children and how much their own universe depended upon trusted, loving hands. Positive rays of mind control are based on love, and responsible parents are an integral part of a healthy future generation. If an indifferent parent chooses to give their rights to others, this creates a cesspool of neglect and physical, mental, and sexual abuse. At the end of the day, if we look at the time factor and life in general, school age is the prelude of the formation of an individual's successes and failures.

I am sure we do not need to go terribly far into our own personal affairs to realize the positive effects of caring and understanding parents. Parental affection and interaction after school can help to solve a child's problem. What a moral boost it is to have a father sit beside his child and exchange his knowledge with him or her and develop an understanding of his child. These moments of truth were what we all had to undergo while we were facing our own development.

What makes these feelings vanish for our unwanted generation? What created the shift in understanding we grew up with? The answers to these questions are extensive and harsh. I will name a few of them, and I am sure you will be able to come up with some of your own. Those that come to my mind are too many distractions, too many bloody games, too many disrespectful games, too many prejudiced games, too much time watching television, too much time judging and condemning in video games.

These can be legitimate good times, but I want to point out some of the reasons why children become unwanted or drop out of school. There are of course some opportunists who choose these avenues in their adolescence to befriend a child to influence their way of thinking. At the end of the day, it is a cesspool of bad examples and bad attitudes that entrap children. Cartoons from decades ago are nothing like what children gobble every day in today's society. Some of the cartoons are innocent, but can we honestly affirm this for all of them?

The reason why I boldly question these avenues is not because these legitimate things are bad but because we are the fruit of our own destiny. Nothing can be erased or changed in one factor of the education we might allow our future generation to grow with. I believe we have to focus more on the responsibility of learning how to become responsible. This would create a fair and adequate balance in our system of education.

The benefit of communicating and understanding creates an atmosphere of pride and loyalty while developing trust and love between parents and their children. That chain between educations is called trust, and it is the link between children and their parents in time of need. Children have the right to know they are safe, and if anything, they don't like comes their way, they know they have loving and trustworthy parents. Trust has many areas in the giant universe of knowledge under the umbrella of love, faith, generosity, and above all, responsibility of adults and parents.

Education and indoctrination are two different avenues. It is the responsibility of adults to make the difference when referring to the subject of education. If we don't have the courage to analyze the difference between good learning and the smell of rotten education, then we will be indoctrinated into believing what is being indoctrinated in us. I am not saying the whole system of education is rigged and becomes an automatic source for indoctrination. I have tried to amplify the risks our next generation would be exposed to because of the negligence of parents.

We need an approved legal system of education where good manners and relationships are adequately taught. Children won't stay children forever. During our time as children, we were exposed to so much variance in good or bad behaviors. We had the opportunity to be exposed to knowledge while living our childhood; future generations need and deserve this beneficence.

I am sure some of the older folks will be tempted to say this young generation is rotting due to the indoctrination by the commodities of technology. Their point of view should be considered. On the other hand, progress in society is measured by the innovation coming from individuals forming society. In a way, technology is a vital means for society to grow, from humans working the earth to having a superior knowledge and capacity.

Having said this, it is also good to keep in mind that we need to respect all activities and careers in the world. For some, farming is their choice, and for others, technology is their choice. It is not technology in itself that is the problem; the problem comes when a combination of exploitation and technology work as a pair toward indoctrination. There is a lot more to write on this subject, but I have to limit myself because I have other chapters to cover. While this is a small presentation of reasons why education is important in our society, we have to keep in mind that education alone is not the total answer.

Children and mind control in our society are a natural benefit when society works in accordance with natural laws dictated by purity, and excellence radiates all over nature. We have to admit there is nothing perfect on Earth, and this is not an excuse to justify cowardly negligence and false trust in an established system. We have the right to choose the avenue we want our children to be vested with by the power of knowledge learned through an honest and truthful system.

It gives us nothing to try to rewrite history into a private agenda of manipulation, exploitation, negligence, and abuse of power. The skeletons in history's closet already overshadow our own existence. It is not by taking the ostrich for a model that history will rewrite itself. Not everyone belongs to the category of "go with the flow"; there are some parents and individuals who are actively involved in their children's future and success.

I will end this chapter by saying, "We reap what we sow." We sleep on the bed we have made for ourselves and the one we make for future generations.

9

PARENTAL RESPONSIBILITIES

IN THIS CHAPTER following children and mind control, I will elaborate on the subject of parental responsibility. I believe it is a good time to explore these responsibilities. One more time, let's use the dictionary of "Parental responsibility Law and Legal definition to fully understand the subject: "Parental responsibility refers to a set of rights and privileges that children have with their parents and with those adults who have a significant role in the child's life as the basis of their relationship.

Usually, parental responsibilities include both parenting time and decision-making responsibilities. When parental responsibilities are determined through the court, the court allows the parent with decision-making responsibility to determine the child's upbringing, including his or her religious training. Usually, responsibility for a minor child must be shared by both parents, unless the court finds that shared parental responsibility would be detrimental to the child.

However, the court can order sole parental responsibility, with or without visitation, when it is in the best interests of the minor child. It is to be noted that before awarding sole parental responsibility, the trial courts are required to make a specific finding of harm to the child."

The definition retrieved from the dictionary on "parental responsibility, law, and legal definition" surprisingly goes hand in hand with the chapter of children and mind control. I am glad to see such a relation between these two different avenues needed for a healthy family to develop. There are two kinds of parenting responsibilities: ones that are governed by love, and ones that are governed by common sense. Love requires flexibility at times and restrictions at others. I want to get into the subject on each of them separately because I believe not all flexibilities and restrictions are perfect. However, we need a fair balance while parents carry out their parental duties.

Love and common sense are two elements actively present in every living species on Earth. Even animals have a specific sense of love and common sense. Take birds, for example. They ensure that their nests are high and hidden from the view of other species. Everything in nature is poised by the knowledge and wonder of love with doses of common sense. Human nature is based on wisdom and knowledge capacity, but these avenues are not gratuitous. Love and common sense, however, are free for the ones who search and reach out for their benefits.

Life is all about success and a means to arrive at a fruitful existence. These two patterns for success are offered to each of us, while an effort on our behalf is required. Positive attitudes in persevering parents can create the perfect grounds for good education and good examples. But first, before going into the benefit of good education and good examples, I will look again into the negativity of the opposite of these wonders in the qualities nature is in charge of reminding us.

When we come into the stage of parenting, we have already learned a sense of responsibility; if we haven't, we are heading straight to catastrophe. Life is set up in a way where we have to find and define the good and the bad elements rendered possible through common sense and judgmental attitudes. In situations where negligence is the norm in a family's education, we notice the inner corps of family values fracturing. Parents don't interact with their own issues, and frankly, how could they if before becoming parents, they neglected their own internal affairs? While young, nature is consistent, although we grown-up humans have a strong tendency to believe we know it all before the future arrives.

This causes problematic situations in a society because facing the uncertainty of each individual's response toward common sense and love. We know we are not responsible for the actions of negligent parents, but as a community, we all have to pay the price. In many cases, after the disaster is already a reality, reflections like, "I should have done this or that differently" or "Next time I won't repeat the same mistake." Most of the time, it is too late to ensure that lessons are learned when irresponsible men or women fail to rectify the problematic situation.

This is where bad parenting takes root. With all the devastating effects of negligence toward the key of life, parents are given a way to success free of charge. Disposition is the only demand asked on the behalf of nature for each of us to enable the power and knowledge of communicating with wisdom. Sometimes bad parenting originates because we like to make things more complicated than they really are, and the result is negligence that follows bad decisions.

The perfect balance and harmony we receive from nature is not totally achievable because we have to constantly adjust. Why do we have to constantly adjust? Because we are experimenting with imperfections in nature, which, at the base, is perfect. Why do we experiment with such troubling situations if nature is perfectly and solidly based? This is because of the phenomenon of "free will" that nature has given us. Nature gave us her vast universe the day we saw the light of this Earth for the first time.

When we scrutinize the negative effects of parenting, we soon discover the importance and presence of negative mind control in education. We come in direct contact with the reality and sadness of what an irresponsible and negligent attitude is capable of producing within society. Some of those negativities are so out of bounds and in direct contradiction with wisdom that they create monsters, criminals, and assassins. We are the fruit of our own destiny and if we choses to live a criminal life style we will leave a legacy of being eternally remembered as vagabonds.

Parenting demands solidifying convictions through good examples. In the case of bad parenting, we face paradoxes of excuses and false pretenses to justify why a coward exists. Once ideology of an excuse is used to blame others for an individual's lack of responsibility, everything becomes justified, even murder. Nothing is capable of rendering individual free choice to render a man or a woman vested with honor while their own choices are not coherent with the demanding aspects of honorable qualification.

In the sadness and the depth of incoherence, multiple abuses are perpetrated against children and adolescents, exposing them to a cesspool of negligence while working their way toward adulthood. This tragedy is exactly what perpetrates the cowardly pretense of projecting their own defiance upon other events that occurred in their developing life. This is a factor a bad situation will engender in other regrettable moments following the long-term consequences. What is not excusable is when irresponsible parents project their crime of negligence upon another's legacy.

As always, there are two sides to a coin. It is the same concept when we enter the domain of parental education while in preparation of becoming parental. This does not happen overnight but in harvesting time and willingness in order to acquire a sense of responsibility.

Negligence results in nothing good in a society because it is the opposite of prosperity and provides no good examples of dedication. In this case, the ostrich strategy is seen as a source of potential danger, surpassing wisdom while digging a hole to blind its view from imminent danger. It is not because we occasionally find a rotten apple on an apple tree that it is justified to cut down the whole three. With every bad apple, there are one hundred good apples on the same tree.

Parenting is nothing to gamble with because our next generation's future will be in grave danger. For selfish parents, nobility and dignity do not take part in their personal affairs, and thus a chaotic education becomes the norm. These individuals arrive at negligence as they get older; they do not have to suffer from the consequences of their choices.

Now I will walk into the positive field and benefits of good parenting. What an honor for parents to hold in their hands the fruit of love that they have marvelously procreated from their own flesh and blood. The moment a child is held in the loving arms of its mother, a whole universe is enhanced and becomes more vibrant because this little baby is the continuation of the circle of life. Good parenting is something we are never totally ready for because each day that has been will never be the same.

There are many variants in time and situations that play a key role in the achievement of being able to mature as we progress in life and responsibilities. Good parenting starts with the examples we receive from our parents and also the closest friends to our parents. It is a subject that we are constantly discovering every day. New techniques are being discovered and adjustments are being made. To be a good parent requires a disposition to use our qualifications to discern good and bad while taking care of our responsibilities.

Good parenting is the key toward great rewards, such as children developing a moral compass that is identical to their parents' beliefs and examples. There will never be two identical individuals, but one good example will create a positive avenue for the observant child. Parenting is little steps taken from our own parents to reproduce the same effect, and a little step each of us has had to make while under the umbrella of our parental love and care.

The fruit of good parenting is the gratitude for the parents and for the society where parental responsibilities are the wonder of nature revealing itself. Children are precious, just as they were before we began to parent, and we have to remember we have had the same conditions and circumstances that our children face today. If good parenting is sound and present, children are blessed with knowledge living under the loving umbrella of wisdom where they commute between their parents' love and their education.

Sure, nothing is perfect and the pretentious idea of a perfect environment and love will never be a reality. The more a child is exposed to good parenting, the more guarantee that child has to become successful by retrieving examples from their loving and caring parents. Trust is a basic security toward the evolution of good parenting in connectivity with good examples and love.

Take away the environment of trust, and the result could be a deadly situation. Children know they are vulnerable, and they depend upon their parents' generosity and care. To a certain extent, they expect that this will be given to them. The moment this expectation is fulfilled, a strong foundation of good education becomes sound and vital. Good parenting involves interacting with the children. In doing so, trust is built, where children know that if they have a moment of difficulty or are in need, they have a strong advocate looking out for them.

As we take in the wonder of becoming a parent, new visions and understanding arrive if we truly follow the laws of nature, wisdom, and common sense. These three steps cannot be escaped or ignored without serious consequences. Parental responsibility is the foundation of future generations in order for them to grow and preserve their identities. As children receive the positivity of a responsible parent, they not only move toward the evolution of a future adult but they are also planted with a sense of responsibility.

When we see a child or a baby, we acknowledge the eventual adult in its most vulnerable form. Most of the time, we have a smile on our face when we see these figures, and most likely we say or think, "Look at this little face!" When children reaching adulthood are educated and groomed under bad parenting, they portray the image we have provided for our own generation and society. That same face becomes a criminal when proven guilty under brutal evidence of criminal offenses, and we are the first ones to condemn that little smiling face.

There are some exceptions, such as when the child had a perfect opportunity in his or her life but chose to ignore the good examples of his or her parents. This bizarre situation could be due to many factors, one being that he or she is badly influenced by jealous and envious close friends. It could also occur because of personal choices to directly revolt against something or someone that the child considered an abuse of power instilled by control-freak parents. In this case, the child's vision is distorted, and his or her understanding is still in the developmental stage, blinded by desire to get even with his or her parents.

There are also perfect opportunists constantly running around the neighborhood looking for innocent children to trap into a life of misery and dishonesty. One may ask, "What do these ideas have to do with good parenting?" The answer is simple: good parenting is the opposite of exploitation on underage children. Good parenting is a weapon to defeat any negative circumstances when a child reaching adulthood becomes at odds with the sad reality of becoming a criminal. Above all, while parental responsibilities are in demand, expectations from children should always be guided and instructed by love.

Good administration guided by vigilance is the refuge that guarantees trust and conversation with our children. Quality trust is the basis of communication. Sometimes a word of encouragement, even a warning, signals vigilance that promotes safety and trust in our world. To a certain degree, we can honestly say we are the creators of our future generations. This creation will be either a proud extension of distinguished descendants or worthless and unwanted vagabonds. The choice belongs to the responsible parents to plant the seeds of trust and love while preparing their children for the future.

When it comes to parental responsibilities, there are so many little details at play that parents must take one detail at a time as necessary. To be a good parent can be very stressful, and sometimes it results in ungrateful children. In all circumstances, love will always debunk negativity. When we begin parenting, we have to face the reality that we are either the continuance of our principles or the devastating consequences of our cowardice.

There is nothing to be negligent about or to gamble with because at the end of our lives, we will have a positive or negative eternal remembrance for generations to come. We are unable to rewrite the history of our presence in this world; however, we have the opportunity to seal wonders of success in dignity and labor. The next generation will measure education and parenting responsibilities and dispositions when they access their inheritance.

I will end this chapter with the utmost reverence to the entire parental community—those who raise their families to adhere to the laws of common sense and loyalty. These are the individuals whose names will be forever written in the book of world history as predominant and faithful, who have contributed in creativity and wonder. Parenting is the most challenging task individuals can undertake.

Love engulfs the seed of respect, education, and tenderness, which, above all, creates true devotion. With love, every situation is a win because love is patient, love is kind, love is reverent, and above all, love is the perfect example to generations in their footsteps toward appreciation and success.

We have discussed the positive and negative scenarios of parenting responsibilities. As we progressed into the subject, contrasts were noticed and clearly demonstrated. One avenue led to wonderful experiences, while the other avenue was conducive to self-destruction, low-class individuals, vagabonds, and criminals.

The choices are clearly ours, and no one can claim responsibility for our actions. We cannot project our ultimate duties onto someone else. Once love has done its work, it is our responsibility to act in a responsible manner and with pride because we are the fruit of love and not hazardous individuals.

10

LIVING WITHOUT A MENTORSHIP

W E ALL HAVE to find a prime reason for our existence. Like it or not, we created our own paradox. Because of free will, we can choose any avenue to conduct our affairs.

Our existence is made of two opposite forces that work together simultaneously; this seems impossible, but it is actually true and possible. We experiment with two forces in every situation we encounter, and this gives us the possibility to achieve two things that are opposite to each other with opposite consequences.

This statement seems to say two opposite things; nevertheless, we live in a magnetic field where we encounter good sources and evil sources. This is why, at one point or another, we have to cap our destiny and accept the consequences of our choices. This chapter is the continuation of the importance of good parenting responsibilities. Mentorship for responsible parents is an education in which more experienced and knowledgeable parents help guide less experienced and less knowledgeable parents.

Responsible parents are individuals who teach and give sound advice to their children, leading the way by example and encouragement. Responsible parents also develop a partnership between their vast field of experience and their child who wants to learn. Good expertise from devoted parents provides the child with trusted counselors, especially in occupational settings where love requires vigilance and awareness. Parental mentoring is a process of informal transmission in knowledge, social capital, and psychosocial support, the results of which are measured by the pride of a responsible parent.

Responsible parents sharing their experience in structured education affect the amount of psychosocial support, career guidance, and role modeling occurring in the mentoring education in which the children and parents are engaged. Responsible mentoring is relationship based, and it is a process that always involves communication. When the children receiving mentorship get older, they may be referred to as protégés. When time goes on, the children reach adulthood, find their way to university, and become an apprentice and/or a mentee.

Life without a mentorship in youth is like a vessel without any safety provided in case of a disaster. Parents are like a life vest for their children's future when they follow in the footsteps of prior wisdom, trusted advisers, and guidance. In order to have the opportunity for our children to find motivation in their life, they have to be exposed to a positive ray of mentorship. Where would this positive ray of mentorship come from if the parent does not provide a secure, trusting, and loving home? Most likely not from an outsider of the family—this is where plenty of risks have been taken with lots of disastrous results.

It is an honor for parents to be given a unique opportunity to act as a mentor for their flesh and blood. They serve as trusted counselors and loving teachers, especially in occupational orientations for later when, in due time, a prosperous setting and future goals are set for their children. Because of free choice, children becoming adults are free to take advice from their parents or to ignore their warnings. This is where wisdom comes in and can be used to regulate how parents approach their children. There are two outcomes when children consider accepting or rejecting the rays of parental mentorship. The first outcome would be great success for the eventual adult who chooses to abide by the mentorship of his or her parents. The second outcome would be a continuous break down and a torrent of despair that will guide the future adult into an abyss of negligence.

I am sure everyone has, at one time or another, heard this saying: "When I was born, I didn't know anything. When I reached six years, Mom and Dad knew everything. When I reached eleven years, I started to doubt whether Mom and Dad knew something. When I reached fifteen years, I started to question whether Mom and Dad knew something. When I reached eighteen years, Mom and Dad knew absolutely nothing. When I reached my older age, I came to realize that Mom and Dad knew something, but by then it was too late, and they were no longer with me." This makes perfect sense when a parent takes the role of communicator on behalf of their children, who are vulnerable and lacking in experience. In order to make a positive impact on their children, future parents have to learn how to become their own mentor. Discipline is required for any existing family and business if they wish to prosper and be in good standing with the products they offer society. If one ounce of lack of respect exists toward discipline, then an inevitable collapse would be an imminent reality.

There are four categories in the domain of discipline. The first category is love; the second is experience; the third is perseverance; the fourth is consequences. Discipline is a training that is expected to produce a specific character or pattern of behavior, especially in producing moral or mental improvement. Love comes from the loving exchange of a parent to ensure a balance in the demand of conformation while imposing discipline. The positive side of good discipline makes children respectful, watchful, and orderly.

This has, for effect, plenty of wonders of wisdom to rise and bloom, sending a signal of a healthy and disciplined future that generations will glorify and advocate. We need a fair balance of disciplined, loving hands to create positivity in the development of character. It is unfortunate that parents sometimes neglect to discipline their children; this can result in opening doors for opportunists to ravage the innocence of these children. I am sure the first thing that comes to mind when talking about discipline is austerity.

What is austerity? It is a condition of living without unnecessary things, without comfort, without money or goods; it is a practice, habit, or an experience that is typical of control freaks. Distances from each other are mistaken and misjudged, placed onto the same level, set in categories of abuse of power or control of the environment. This is where wisdom comes in hand to counteract the negative implication we attribute to discipline. In every situation and government regulation, there are forms of discipline approved by laws and regulations.

Putting discipline and austerity side by side is a grave mistake. This is dangerous for society because we all need forms of discipline to abide by rules and laws. If parents are unable to establish discipline while educating their children, then the family will dissolve. Perfectly balanced regulations are not achievable, but a near balance of regulations is workable. The notion of love guides parents' common sense. Common sense allows parents to discern and prevent any counterattacks from others. This is the beginning of acquiring wisdom.

Children have so much to adjust to while in their child-hood, and therefore it would be unfair to expect them to perfectly model their parents' guidance. Parents guided by wisdom will realize in due time that their children are bound to make errors, just like any of us adults. If they make an error as a future adult, it is not because they had a faulty beginning in life. It becomes a fair justification to mentally disfigure the esteem of the child into a representation of a monster. In doing so, parents who rush to use discipline to rectify a problem will devastate the child. In situations like this, the child would choose to close down any openness he or she had with the parents.

We all need a positive boost coming from the loving hearts of parents to anchor good manners and respectful dispositions toward the educational exchange between chil-dren and parents. By doing our part in providing a good example to our children, we will discover our own imper-fections, and this, in many cases, becomes a game changer. What game changer am I referring to? I am referring to how we will perceive our children's moment of weakness versus how long it takes us to possess the knowledge we have acquired over time.

This would be the result of wisdom, if we have given wisdom and common sense a chance to imprint their quali-ties in ourselves during our adolescence. Wisdom works in parallel with mentorship when children come to discover this wonder of nature and maintain it. The growth in intel-ligence and self-esteem goes beyond the expected result because wisdom gives children a sense of deep pride and responsibility. Parents are at ease to navigate a fertile and promising ground by laying a solid foundation to modify and solidify the interests of their child.

Is it possible to live without a mentorship or a secret goal? I guess it is possible; however, two outcomes with dire consequences are to be expected. First, we face the chance that realities and hardship will be enough to shape negligent individuals. Sometimes hardships are the wake-up call that follows a willpower to interact with responsiveness. But most of the time, by then, it is a harder chore to tackle. However, it is not impossible to demand more dedication and willingness to snap out of the cesspool the individual chose to experiment in.

Unfortunately, once a child is damaged by bad habits and negligence on the behalf of parents or on their own behalf, this becomes, in multiple cases, a hopeless case. In this scenario, we are confronted with results directly related to a ruined life navigated without solid principles. The gathers are infested with negligent adults who are the faulty party to how a whole generation will be affected. Unfortunately, we will notice children with these indifferent attitudes toward responsibility. These children are the ones who will bear the burden of abuse and molestation and be deprived of human dignity. Unwanted as humans in their daily struggle, they reject their consecutive experience of abuse and molestation.

These are the consequences of a lack of mentorship and motivation, which directly results in adults ruining their future and the futures of the following generations. Basically, in life there are two choices: to be a considerate and responsible individual vested with the power and knowledge of wisdom, or to live under a bridge and blame the whole world for one's situation. Individuals who make the second choice will find multiple excuses to fabricate an event following real trauma to justify their stance toward life in general.

For the children, these are the shenanigans of multiple sources influenced by cruelty, anger, irresponsibility, and negligence, deprived from the right to be exposed to a solid and trustworthy mentorship. These children, for the most part, fall into the category of victimization. They even lose their lives after so many doors are open to inconceivable atrocities. Some of these children will be a rare exception and will do everything in their power to interact with common sense. These children will be smart enough to reject the false promise of maintaining their individual responsibility to others.

These children will succeed in life, while the others succumb to the heavy load of depression, anxiety, and low self-esteem. Such children regard their presence in this universe as a waste deserving of a vagabond's lifestyle. This is the sad consequence of adults and parents neglecting to rectify personal wrongdoing. This is where society as a whole has to pitch in and foot the bill because wisdom has compassion toward these children. However, wisdom does not have the power to rectify or change bad behaviors on behalf of the depraved adults, whose only goals are to live day by day.

We have to make choices about our future and how we want the next generation to remember our time spent here in this universe. Children are the continuation of the circle of life, and if the heart of life is broken, how will we be able to find a good cure to heal the wound imposed on them? Families are the precious basis of every child who sees the light of this Earth. If he or she is given false representations of the family institution, and time allows him or her to reach adulthood, then would it be possible to undo a bad start in their life?

Some may argue that the parents in question must have encountered difficult issues during the time they had to depend on a loving parent. Choices of prior parents are the same for the parent who chose to neglect their children under the pretense of having been deprived to interact with their loving and caring parent. There are no excuses for negligence when it comes time to educate the next generation. This becomes a duty for all parents to become responsible. Since we all don't have the same start in life, the teenage years allow us to mature first before teaching the next generation how to evolve.

By doing so, we will soon discover the power of wisdom helping to create a system where positive mentorship is diffused at the best abilities and requirements. This step, however, is not an easy task. An entire future generation is at risk when parenting individuals have tarnished maturity. This faulty part of some parents neglecting to provide mentorship does not become a token for other parents to follow in the footsteps of destructive environments.

Are we able to live without mentorship? I believe we are not able to coexist without some form of disposition toward mentorship. Why do I believe we cannot exist without good or bad mentorship? Because nature is providing us free choice to choose our avenues and legacies.

It is impossible to rectify others' errors and negligence. We are our own authors of a fruitful existence or a lamentable one in calamity and self-demolition. Just as there is only one captain steering the wheel of a ship, we are the only ones in a position to sail our vessel. In an agitated storm, it takes some time for a captain to gain expertise. It is the same scenario when we navigate our own ship. We are free to load what we choose onto the carrier and free to guide our vessel toward its final destination.

There is no guarantee we will be able to navigate our vessel in a calm ocean. We might experience some turbulence; perhaps it is the perfect condition for a hurricane. This is where wisdom interacts with mentorship and serves as a lighthouse, shining a ray of light for the captain to adjust his vessel toward the brilliant reflection leading into the port.

Children are the most vulnerable in our society, and they are forever set to become the beginning of all sources leading to success, or they are forever set to fall under the spell of audacities leading to a negligent and disastrous manner of living.

I will conclude this chapter with a personal vision about the importance of good mentorship and the devastating consequences we come in contact with when we neglect to interact with positive education. When we have positive exposure to mentorships as a family living under the umbrella of wisdom and diligence, we experience a marvelous production and wonder. The most precious power given in this universe is the ability to create a family. To have been given the opportunity to experiment with the power of unity through the links of a wise family opens the door to more communication and good behavior. We are allowed to belong to only one family, and this one chance is the prelude of an entire wonder of existence.

Now here is my last thought in this chapter regarding ruined opportunities following bad education and negligence due to bad parenting: our children will always be our legacy, no matter what excuses we may make. Love them or not, they will forever mark our flesh and bone. Falsely trying to justify our response to a bad situation in our personal life will not take away the burden of sad realities that our response would impose onto our children. We as parents will be forever remembered as the future generation that will remember their prior generation. It is like a chain; once you pick up the first links, the whole chain follows in its entirety, either in preserved condition or in an ugly reality.

Frankly, no one can survive without having some kind of a dream, and while living one's adolescence, not all dreams are good. Parents have unique opportunities to help the good dreams of their children to emerge by ensuring they destroy the bad dreams with good examples and loving care.

11

PREVENTING NEGATIVE MIND CONTROL

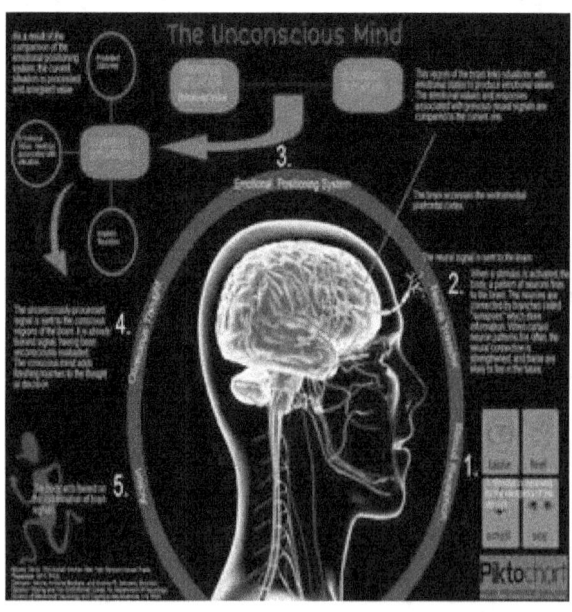

I N ORDER TO prevent something, we have to acknowledge the possibility of it occurring in good deeds or offensive manners. We are incapable of recognizing wrong avenues whose birth might come from non-premediated if our stance toward good intending open doors to ambiguities. To prevent means to keep something from happening. Prevention is reserved for those interventions that occur before the initial onset of disorder.

What does prevention include? Preventive intervention creates actions to target the general public with selective interventions; instruction is also a clear message for prevention. For example, responsible parents target the education of their children while under their care. Future generations target the living testimonies of success or the total disasters following either positive or negative mind control. Prevention is a system that achieves, through the application of multiple strategies, an ongoing process that must relate to each emerging generation.

Negative mind control takes many forms and styles to disfigure the beauty of the human race and render this wonder of nature an undesirable monster. What does nonchalance include? It plants false ideologies in beliefs that everything is fine, and no one should be forced to accept good lessons and examples from exemplar teachers. This stance becomes an open door that works directly against laws of common sense and wisdom.

What does prevention guidance include? It includes general public daily activities that have not been identified on the basis of individual risks. This creates preventive interventions for high-risk individuals who are identified as having minimal but detectable signs of doubtful symptoms. These groups of individuals may not fully meet the diagnostic levels at the present times when they make the choice to

cap the ceiling of their lives. Operational prevention influences and promotes constructive lifestyles and norms that
discourage bad behaviors, such as the use of drugs.

What is the definition of positive operational prevention?
Promotion of good parenting skills strengthens the family
as their first defense against any form of abuse. It is building academic and vocational skills that allow individuals the
potential to develop into contributing members of society. It
also raises awareness of the dangers of drug use and the benefits of constructive behavior. Providing trustworthy skills in
parental mentoring will achieve positive role modeling for
youth. Building social skills enables the development of a
strong self-image that leads to positive life decisions.

What are the basic prevention strategies? Mobilizing
communities to establish environments that enhance
positive personal development and also establishing and
strengthening policies that promote healthy lifestyles,
which become community norms. Is it possible to banish
negative mind control? I don't see this happening. We navigate in a sea of good and evil forces that mark our stance
while we choose how we will conduct ourselves.

Does a sea of evil become a valuable justification in
letting evilness run rampant in our society? For the negligent, this becomes the reason for their existence because
they often are too busy blaming others for their misfortune. Blaming others for personal wrongdoings works in
pair with negligence, which finds its justification in comparisons. This becomes the typical agenda unveiled by each
of these negligent individuals who believe the whole world
owes them a living. No effort is required from their point

of view; they will, however, spend their time making themselves inept while creating their handicaps.

Losers become, by their free choice, a waste of themselves and are considered disgraceful by loyal and honest society members who are forced to foot the bill of these negligent partisans. The nonchalant justify their negligence by blaming the cowardice of others. No one is excluding their parents from mistakes since anyone is forced to imitate the bad examples showed to them. Courage and determination are the key remedies to create a world without negative mind control, and it demands from each of us some effort to learn how to become responsible.

We create our own wonders when we live in an environment of trust among one another, and we also portray a miserable relationship with each other in chaotic situations. Laws and regulations will serve only to solidify citizens' common sense, annexing personal good or bad experiences for the global common causes. It is important for us to remember a good society abides by the principles and norms of wisdom. How do we define fruitful endowment of positive norms implemented through the knowledge of wisdom?

Norms refer to the authoritative standards that serve to model principles of the rights and actions that bind the members of a society in order to guide, control, and regulate proper behavior. Eventually it becomes the daily standard of development and achievement deriving from the average achievement of a large group. That large group mentioned could be considered the sheep who don't care about dignity and prosperity. These sheep are mentally programmed through the medium of television and news.

Sheep do not have a pattern or trait typical for the good behavior of a social group; rather, they have the traits of negligent individuals. They personally chose to split away from honorable practice, procedure, or custom, and instead chose negligence as their norm. A healthy society is proudly ratified by wisdom's reign, creating a solid ground toward the fertilization of virtues in positive mind control.

Keeping in mind the end result of a positive attitude toward a zero tolerance of negativity is enough for wisdom to harmoniously enhance the whole universe. Global success always gets help from the components of the global beneficiary assimilating cost-effective results. The opposite point of failure due to neglecting responsibilities is done individually and alone nonchalant choices become crucial momentum. I am trying to portray the possibilities we possess to create zero tolerances toward negativities. I know it is easier to visualize products of the image we attempt to create.

Determination and faith in good morality are the chores of enriching cultures transmitting different results of positivity in our society. We are the products of our own choices; time and effects will be our judge because we live in a combination of time and effects. Playing the ostrich defense mode will not make our society the model of morality for generations to come. Every day we are given the opportunity to interact positively with each other, and this becomes the wisdom we create for future generations.

Negativity steers sheep toward a lamentable, dysfunctional, and hateful system employed by a handful of opportunists. These monsters care only about their own ends and eventually lead individuals to abuse drugs. Why do people use alcohol and drugs?

There are many reasons why individuals come to accept alcohol and drugs as the curator of invincible obstacles:

- Curiosity
- Indoctrinated belief that alcohol and drugs are not harmful
- Mind-set believing that drugs alleviate symptoms of depression
- To cope with false pretenses following traumatic experiences
- Attempt to relieve childhood sexual abuse or school failures
- Sensation-seeking behavior
- Substance use by family members
- Peer pressure
- Belief that it is a community norm
- Exposure to pro-use message in mass media
- Access and availability

Now let's take a look at the effects on the brain when drugs are used:

Paranoia	Addiction
Aggressiveness	Impaired judgment
Hallucinations	Impulsiveness
Behavioral problem	Loss of self-control

Abuse of nicotine, cocaine, and marijuana affects the brain's "reward" circuit, which is part of the limbic system. Initially, individuals might be using drugs as a cry for relief under depressive modes as they lose the ability to think before acting. These individuals underestimate the power of drugs to alter their brain chemistry and interfere with their ability to make decisions. Problematic situations follow overdoses of these substances. The intake of drugs can cause injury, death, illness, and disability. Substance abusers become vulnerable to preventable death and to domestic violence.

Now let's take a look at alcohol abuse. Not everyone will experience the detrimental effects from one or two servings of alcohol a day. This level of consumption may even decrease the risk of cardiovascular disease and dementia. The following list outlines the short- and short-term effects of alcohol abuse.

Short-term effects:

Cardiovascular disease	Lowered reflexes
Dementia	Poor coordination
Relaxation	Slowed activity of the brain
Reduced inhibitions	

Long-term effects:

Cirrhosis of the liver	Death of brain cells
Pancreatitis	Brain disorders
Cardiac arrhythmias	Lowered mental function
Liver damage	Tolerance
Nerve damage	

When someone reaches a tolerant level, he or she becomes dependent. Addiction to alcohol becomes a deadly disease for a majority of addicted individuals. When alcohol dependency takes root, the body cannot function without alcohol. A sad reality of abusing alcohol is that it affects certain neurotransmitters of the brain. The brain becomes accustomed to the way that alcohol affects these brain chemicals. The result is that the brain can no longer send proper signals to the rest of the body without the presence of alcohol.

Once someone has developed a dependence on alcohol, he or she will continue to drink regardless of any serious physical symptoms related to alcohol consumption. A person who has developed alcohol dependence will drink even if he or she suffers social or personal loss. Sometimes alcohol addiction will lead to loss of a job or career, breakup in a personal relationship, and the worst scenario: an arrest for unlawful behavior related to alcohol consumption.

I will end this chapter on a positive note. We possess the internal power and the remedy to conquer weakness with the power of wisdom. Not everyone has to be classified as a negligent individual when they receive a helping hand. This would be totally unfair for the less fortunate. There are many people in our society who simply cannot help but to seek help from healthy society. If the possibility to acquire autonomy was presented to these individuals, I am positive they would gladly take it.

Wisdom recognizes the difference between a person with a handicap whose life has been shadowed with misfortune and a citizen who simply innovates excuses to appear to be disabled. There has to be a fair balance in societal systems that lets generosities go toward the less fortunate, while the pretentious debunk and expose. I know there will always be exploitation done on the behalf of lazy crooks, but the majority of loyal workers will criticize and point outraged fingers at their audacious work.

12

MONEY TALKS; MIND CONTROL WALKS

CENTURIES HAVE SERVED to draw the line between the power of money and the vigilance of good orators to keep power under one roof. We will be subject to intimidation and extortion as long as opportunists will find occasion to exploit and control their knowledge and power. Can money really talk? Sure it can, although money made of paper represents possession or abilities to acquire goods.

Control is a psychological state where an individual's normal personality is replaced by another's. Sometimes justice is served, but it is more like injustice. The more you retrieve from a system, the more global you tend to become. Taking control or occupancy of properties without regard to honest ownership allows dictatorships to emerge. Not all controlled money travels the same way. Money possesses many faces, shapes, and personalities.

Some individuals refuse to be questioned by inquiries or to be investigated if their control and power was acquired by fraud. This is where money talks. When individuals are in that position, the lives of others become worth less than a penny. From emperors to presidents, the authorities we follow make the trail of the silenced coming from money. We would be astonished by the connection between money and power. They work hand in hand.

History repeats itself under different personalities, figures, principles, promises, extortions, and lies. And persuasion makes them believable. The negotiations between power, money, control, and authority are usually the culprit behind a hidden scene where the general public is not welcomed or wanted. Secrets surround a universe of potential abuse of power and money by the dictations of globalists. To this day, how many sudden disappearances and suicidal mysteries originate from knowledge and power?

No one can really find an answer to this question because of fears of reprisals from sources that may have connections apart from the person chosen to be a hit man. If, by chance, money-laundering secrets are revealed, the individual(s) in question will investigate where the leaks may have occurred. The reprisals for such acts of negligence can range from sudden death, loss of reputation (being portrayed as unfit to interact with society), and loss of esteem.

There are cases where prisons become the new home for destitute individuals until trust is restored. No longer do these unfaithful individuals consider living a treat after having rendered honorable treatment. However, most of the time, these individuals' "careers" are over and no longer needed, and they might even be running for their lives. Although money made of paper does not have the ability to maneuver travel, technically speaking, the influence of money does travel miles from the original place because of individualism.

This is where we enter into a secret universe where opportunists consult for profits the kingdom where money talks and mind control walks. Multiple victims have been silenced by death, and they return to haunt their murderers. We do not hear about this because mind control governs the secrets of this universe. Some may know about different circumstances taking placing, but they refuse to reveal their knowledge because of fear. There are serious consequences that come from a system where manipulation of money corrupts the sanity of humans.

Ultra-secret organizations are set in place where secrecy is the link between the cover up and money. Opportunists are so secretive that these links that are common in society are not fully present to those around them. Many refuse to believe or acknowledge that shadowed skeleton rules their daily life, until time reveals strategies of taking life. Of course, these organizations have all their documents and master plans destroyed, so they won't be exposed to the general public. Reprisal, slander, physical attacks, and even torture are used in these circumstances.

Wars become the ultimate means of regulating and repairing the damage caused by the exposure of certain individuals where money has corrupted integrity. Slavery took new forms and tactics, so we no longer see anyone in the field forced to work long hours as we witnessed in the history of our universe. Money has become the new form of slavery because it controls everything. Selfish opportunists do as they please while being inspired by succeeding in implanting regulations, rules, and demands on ordinary workers.

Generations follow each other, and every member of that generation bends to the rules and demands of the money-talking expectation. I'm not saying there is something wrong in possessing money—far from it; we are all in need of money to live! In this chapter, I am trying to expose elements and possibilities where money has become the source of revenue for opportunists. I know there will be some critics secretly or openly disgusted about the direction of this chapter.

My intention is not to target any of these organizations or individuals but to shed light on the potential means and ways they use money in our modern world. People with corrupt power are not held accountable for their actions. These individuals know how to obstruct the justice system to protect their rights. Often individuals are baffled because they follow the consequences of culprits who ignore the laws and regulations.

It is not wrong to seek and accept an honestly earned advancement in life. What causes disorder is when opportunists act as providers of goods and promoters of egocentric, hidden agendas through calculated ideologies. Promotions are tests of character, not an assessment for exploitation where the heroism of others is lawfully stolen from its original source. Adversity is hard for individuals living in society, but for the one who handles prosperity, there would be a hundred who would stand adversity.

At times there will be an apparent balance of powers mixed with deplorable, disgraceful, and twisted signals of abuses on behalf of the opportunists' egocentrism. The problem is not the power versus the opportunity; rather, the problem is a combination of empowerment and exploitation through individuals' thirst for money and power. Power and opportunity work as a pair in the field of prosperity. However, they become opposite when the abused become the source of lamentable destructions caused by gluttony.

Having access to money or power does not automatically render an individual a monster or evil; it simply creates opportunities to become imperative. We need wealth and wealthy individuals for a flourishing society; therefore, the issues start when access to money and power become dangerously intolerable for the disadvantaged. Wealth can also create a system where individuals, either by pressure or willingness, arrive to be dependent upon these powers. There are also situations where money and power create jealousy and comparisons when these two come together; it opens an avenue to verbal arguments or physical wars.

A perfect balance between money and power is obviously not reachable; the only achievement we could strive for is excellence in our endeavors to follow the trail of money and power. There will always be rich individuals, along with middle-class and poor individuals, in the composition of society. This does not justify wrongdoing in these three categories, nor does it amplify the positive results of wisely governed money and power. What does magnify the results is the disposition and openness in both camps, rich and poor.

The poor have to recognize that their situation does not always depend upon bad management of power and money on behalf of the rich. Sometimes, the poor voluntarily become destitute by their own negligence and faults caused by jealousy and envy of others' possessions, with little concrete action to change. There are self-created situations where the poor will always be left without owning anything because they lack the disposition and willingness to pay the price to become healthy members of society.

Individual substance in a society means that occupants of a community have to create a disposition that defines the positive or negative ways a person views his or her own world. This brings a contrast of characters that reveals and determines inner morals and values, serving as a reflection of the personality of each individual. If, as individuals, we are cheerful and happy, others will see us as having a sunny disposition. Choosing the direction of our dispositions reveals positive or negative power to render decisions. It becomes relevant in the domain of evaluation of self-control of good or bad dispositions.

Dispositions eventually reveal characteristics of a predominant attitude and the tendency of one's spirits that define specifically one individual's mental and emotional well being, outlook, or mood. At this level, disposition becomes a state of mind regarding something projected toward personal responsibilities while conducting internal affairs. A good attitude produces wonder in an individual's dispositions, helping to develop the positively crafted plan, followed by the concrete success of that individual's choice of actions.

The opposite occurs for negligent attitudes where legitimate excuses are developed from a false attitude of "the whole world owes me a living." From that point of view, the individual choosing this avenue has the tendency to blame others, especially the rich, for his or her misfortunes or errors. It is never the fault of the person who has rejected his or her duties toward himself or herself. The "never my fault" disposition leads to an indifferent attitude where false justifications and jealousy groom remarkably selfish people. Once individuals reach this stage where their attitude becomes comfortable, healthy members of society perceive this as ego-centered.

When individuals depart from the conduct expected of a reasonable and prudent individual, their actions split away from common sense and regulation of wisdom. The concept of a reasonable person distinguishes negligence from intentional acts, such as assault and battery. The hypothetical and reasonable person provides an objective by which the conduct of others is judged. A majority of people active in a community may behave in certain ways that do not establish the standard of conduct within the reasonable person.

Laws and judgments establish how everyone should behave in situations that might pose a threat or harm to the public. These factors include the knowledge and perception from a person actively engaging with physical characteristics as well as all circumstances surrounding that individual activity. Even though groups of people in a community may behave a certain way, this does not establish a standard of conduct reflecting a reasonable person.

Wisdom does not deny personal knowledge of basic facts commonly known in the community. A reasonable person knows that ice is slippery and live wires are dangerous and alcohol impairs driving ability and children might run into the street when they are playing. The prudence of a reasonable individual even takes into consideration a possible lack of knowledge when he or she walks an unfamiliar corridor. The conduct of individuals living in a society must be judged in light of personal knowledge and observations. Reasonable individuals always take this into account.

Finally, a person undertaking a particular activity is ordinarily considered to possess the knowledge common to others who engage in that activity. For example, doctors in a community have to show credentials to the public if they want everyone to trust their knowledge in the medical field. This simple action from higher-educated individuals eradicates some cases where impostors present double personalities. When we talk about money and mind control, every little detail has to be taken into consideration.

A whole of an apple does not represent a half or a quarter of the fruit but its entirety—the perfect original shape of the fruit. Opportunists will always be roaming the streets, trying to entrap individuals with no personal values. Does money talk and mind control walk? Absolutely! Without any doubt, we can affirm that money talks and mind control runs the streets of societies. Money does not personally represent the author of a good deed or the perpetrator of a crime because money does not possess a will. The one using the power of a piece of paper becomes the source of all activities.

Mind power is dynamite for the vulnerable who are intellectually incapable of distinguishing between their rights and the outlaws of exploitation. The ostrich in this case becomes the perfect model and hero of these individuals choosing to ignore warnings from the wisdom of others. Indicators such as gestures and verbal warning signs serve as a means for communicating a troubled time ahead. Total opposite indicators are used as a sequence of digital values whose variations represent coded information. In electronic fields, an indicator represents an impulse or fluctuating quantity as electrical voltage or light intensity whose variations represent coded information.

Today, computers use sequences of digital values whose variations represent coded information. Indicators are used in the fields of sound, image, or messages transmitted or received by means of telecommunication. No matter how you look at the result of the word indicators, every machine comes to a conclusion of different perceptions, receiving and transmitting information.

The point of this chapter is not to guide anyone to a paranoid level. Instead, I want to shed light on the reasons why money talks and mind control walks and expose how they work hand in hand with the manipulation of opportunists helping them in their hidden agenda for money, power, and control. Not everyone is planted with good intentions; even among government officials, opportunists are secretly rampaging and doing so openly. It is so wide open that those pretentious opportunists' arrogance subdues the voice and conscience of those whom they are supposed to be representing.

Having said this, not every member of a government branch will let himself or herself get lectured by these opportunists' hidden agenda. We have to keep in mind the notion of wisdom and the fruit of knowledge in order to prevent deception from trying to gather everyone into a mass field of lies to protect the long life of opportunism. I will end this chapter with motivation about money talking and mind control walking because I believe in giving a fair and equitable chance to both sides.

It will also be good closure upon such subjects where many good events and helping hands have been observed through generosity. Sometimes generosity has sided with personal gain in a well-meaning individual's fortune or reputation because he or she needs to be recognized and acknowledged. His or her behavior creates a bridge between knowledge and ignorance for personal advantage.

Not every action in life should be automatically classified as good or evil; at the same time, actions are expected to be judged according to the individual's intentions.

The more power someone has been entrusted with, the more sources they have to regulate authority. Populations with wealth and morals become rapidly targeted to expose fields of extortion and abuses of power. There are some in power who uphold their oath to protect and conserve citizens' rights. Recognition of good actions creates a chain of events where younger generations witness positive progression through good examples. Their result is more beneficial than their exploitation.

In the world of dominance, the arrogance of selfish opportunists often silences the voices of well-intentioned members of society. We have to pick and choose our avenues, and this will reveal where our moral stand is. No one can do this for individuals; this falls into the domain of principles. There are two main domains when we interact with principles, and they are "good" or "bad" domains. The first works constructively and the second works through sneaky destruction.

13

MENTAL ILLNESS OR MIND CONTROL?

THE TERM "MENTAL illness" defines a state of wellbeing in which an individual realizes his or her abilities cannot cope with the normal stresses of life. Knowledge in the field of mental illness versus mind control has progressed to a level that appropriately differentiates mental illness versus mind control. Although mental health and mind control can be related, they represent different psychological states.

Mental illness collectively diagnosable disorders conditions find results in an individual's actions characterized by alterations in thinking, mood, or behavior. The results of mind control are very similar. The difference is one occurs naturally, and the other is a premeditated state of actions. Mind control can easily take cover under the afflictions of mental illness because they are from the same domain, except there are many categories of mind control treacheries taking form with groomed promises of wellbeing and a perceived life of satisfaction and happiness.

When power and exploitation are rampant, examples of mental illness tend to go up and examples of wisdom tend to vanish into thin air. Evidence shows mental disorders occurring from mind control—especially depressive disorders—and they are strongly related to setting and/or environment. For example, religions use faith, government power, opportunism false promises of happiness.

Since the start of World War II, multiple experiments have nourished globalist agendas and they offer daily substance in today's culture. Many individuals taken in experimentation are dead or presumed vanished, while others are on the path toward self-destruction. This thirst for control and power is relentless. The more power acquired through experimentation, the more power in knowledge never gets satisfied. It seems that when mental illness becomes a promulgation of mind control, the price is the blood of innocent people, leading to the destruction of personality.

There are many forms of destruction created through man-made advertising (i.e., mental control that borders on creating mental illness). Here are some ways advertising is used to promote borderline situations blamed on mental illness:

Indoctrination	Drugs
Persuasion	Manipulations of targets
Dictation	Blanks in recollection
Hallucinations	Late diagnosis of "mental impairments"
Out-of-body experiences	
History of social "unfitness"	Always "too late" to intervene

The list could go on. I chose to name just few of them, and I am sure my readers will be able to come up with some of their own observations. There are also some "mental illnesses" created by self-imposed wrong choices where individuals become addicted to a bad habit. These addictions are legitimate and become the ruin of a brilliant personal capacity to operate in a normal society. A few of these addictions are alcohol, tobacco, and medication, which can lead to eating disorders, pretenses, and denials. I am sure there are more categories of addiction, but this chapter is not about denigration of personal rights. My intention, however, is to offer a wake-up call about defining mental illness versus mind control situations.

What is an addiction? An addiction is a state of enslavement to a habit or practice that becomes psychologically and physically habit forming. Any attempt to cease the use of the substance causes severe trauma. For some individuals attempting to come clean from addictions, the effort will lead them to impairment or to the borderline of mental illness. Addiction comes from the self-acceptance of momentarily finding a form of relief from stress or the reality of personal internal struggles.

Alcohol abuse often takes place because individuals are searching for reasons why bad events in life occur. Alcoholics never find an answer to their question; the next bottle possesses the miraculous answer. It is the same for all legitimate addictions. No matter what enslavement is at the roots, addicts search for a miraculous cure. The effects of these abuses are by far not meeting the hoped results from the individual.

This self-imposed enslavement destroys personal growth, including openness to new experiences, optimism, hopefulness, and purpose in life. Under the influence of their enslavement, individuals find short periods of false answers to their questions. After the effects of alcohol or drugs have dissolved, individuals are brought back to a reality they can now oversee. The result of an addiction directly affects the relationship between an individual choice of enslavement and living in a drug-free society. Drug-free individuals understand their self-worth, their usefulness to society, and their sense of community.

The opposite is true for individuals who follow the laws of enslavement, for they become selfish individuals. Once a system advances through media, ads, and propaganda, disorderly misconduct is the result, and society is astonishingly out of control. Mental illness becomes the popular excuse to come at the defense of the real culprits hidden behind programmed individuals.

Addiction is only a small part of the problems in a socialist system. The other part is the manipulation of opportunists planting the perfect ambiance and program into a nation. Propaganda activists are experts in covering up, especially if a traumatized society is experiencing the effects of unknown circumstances and when the next sudden attack will take place.

There is a fine line that defines mental illness versus a mind-control agenda. That line is often misled by reports and commentary on the behalf of the radio or television station. Every time there is a mass shooting, the mug shots of the culprits of the reprehensible action look similar. The orbit of their eyes is not at their normal position, showing signs of internal distress and confusion. Yet opportunists find excuses to justify the mad man's activities and exploit mentally unstable conditions.

Are these theories reliable and trustworthy? Proposed explanations whose statuses are still conjectural, subject to contrast from well-established propositions that are regarded as reporting matters of actual fact? For the vast majority in society, mind control has already succeeded in creating a blind trust to the hour of news told every day. Theories have become hypothetically workable in a secret society of opportunists who push hidden agendas toward absolute power and control.

The news media, run by the elites, test general propositions that are commonly regarded as the correct version and used as principles for explaining a class of phenomena.

Nothing is more efficient than using a perception of some examples to portray the particular massive presentation. While doing this, they use a system of rules and principles and other methods while acutely reporting live on the developing event.

At this point, general propositions turn into contemplation, speculation, guesses, and conjecture. Reporters speaking behind the microphone are mostly unaware that puppeteers are pulling their strings. A few unsatisfied globalists compose a living skeleton of a snake that crawls like a venomous vampire thirsty for the blood of their next victim.

This is where a limit is drawing in consequences reaching the peak of mental illness versus aftereffect of a spell of destructive mind control. A sobering rhyme from World War II— "loose lips sink ships"—reminds society that the negative effects of mind control create harsh prices in bloodshed on the behalf of innocents. We, as a society, create our own legacy as we lay in the bed we made for ourselves while we seek hours of darkness to refresh us.

Mental illness has nothing in common with terrorist attacks or ideologies planted through the medium of exploitation for the purpose of absolute control. A crime will never be justified by using reason of insanity. Facts and evidence have to corroborate with the specific guidelines of mental deficiencies. If we do not give time to reason and wisdom to intervene, we risk the shameful chance to become our own self-destructive enemies. Mind control is a two-sided sword; one side will stand for wisdom and the other side will lead toward chaos and disorderly manners.

Effective leadership requires sound judgment, good sense, and a strong impulse toward the power of a positive and sane mind. It is important to give impartially governed fields of knowledge by direct understanding of first principles if not by giving a chance for argument. Using the power of wisdom to interact with decisions renders a justification and explanation of a wise decision supporting a belief for action.

Promote healthy reasons while inducing a change of opinion in presentation of arguments standing by reason, to be clear, obvious, and logical with proper justifications. This is an outlook of positive mind control regulated through wisdom and reinforced by individuals who choose the avenue of wisdom. We do not find the need for justification and argument in an orderly chain of events when these actual living conditions are regulated with prudence and wisdom.

Society will respond exactly the way we are presenting our choices when we create positive dedications in our actions toward obliging honor and responsibility. Why are we constantly facing destructive rumors of hate and the internal destruction of family and society? Simply because a majority of societies turned their backs to the benefits wisdom could offer, and they chose to openly run toward the gate of chaos, lies, and deception. Opportunists, in their treachery, covered the well-planned atmosphere under a false pretense of the mental-illness epidemic rampant in society.

We need to analyze every element of sudden chaos if we want to truly remediate the growing problem of insanity taking solid ground in our society. Mental illness has to be reservedly assessed before the final findings of an investigation come to light. I know this involves more than words because writing about a subject never possesses the same effect as dealing with the actual problem. Writing serves as instruction about a subject, and actions are the fruit of learning from quotes read in a book or heard in a presentation.

The results of knowledge depend upon personal involvement with the material and the information we retrieve working toward an agenda of ownership or disgraceful waste. Each individual is responsible for his or her growth and to help establish the laws of common sense. Disorder lives out of negligence and takes root from excuses. It finds longevity in negative examples and survives with nonchalance on behalf of individuals.

A disorderly situation becomes a source of revenue for opportunists because it provides opportunities to bring hope in restoring order in an ongoing cesspool of nonsense. Most of the time, individuals offering help and a caring hand are the ones who are secretly manipulating revenues. There are natural causes where catastrophes erupt from time to time, travel place to place, and create real moments of wonder. When I refer to disorderly situations, I am making allusions to circumstances where a fatal event could have been avoided. Because we have not paid attention to the little details about mental health, the suspect in question has been reported, and victims are decrying the lack of prevention.

Natural catastrophes are not premeditated or groomed; they are acts of nature, and the disorder following the devastation is not toward one specific target. This means the event affects everyone, leaving no one behind. Everyone is served the same dose. There is, however, a fraction between the links of time for everyone in question submitted to natural calamity. There will be the ones who constantly take advantage of others' vulnerabilities and will be the first ones to get back on track. There will be the ones who listen to the voice of wisdom and will soon find relief and prosperity while undergoing a natural disaster. Finally, there will be large numbers of negligent individuals who will choose to stay idle and ask for help.

Life is all about choice, determination, pride, responsibility, and good examples in an effort toward prosperous growth for a healthy society. The opposite remains for the society who chooses to abide by rules regulated by opportunists who do not have any sympathy toward these wastes of life and time. These opportunists will put on a pretense of sympathy and offer a helping hand in return. They will work in secrecy for more power and control.

Mental illness is a natural occurrence and should not be mixed with calamities from individuals who plant opportunities for personal gains. Not all situations are deemed strictly greedy; however, we have to ask wisdom for help in defining which ones are provoked situations versus the ones from natural causes. This will help us to recognize the true nature of an event versus blindly following instructions that, most of the time, are given by the ones who perpetrated a crime.

There is a reason why snakes slither, and the same goes for opportunists while they meet to discuss how to ensnare and subdue the programmed class of individuals. Categories have a great place in their consideration, and their chosen target would most likely be individuals who have already peacefully surrendered. There are two kinds of snakes: ones that are harmless and ones that are poisonous. The harmless snakes do not cause a direct danger like the ones who are poisonous; however, they are both the same snake sneakily slithering on the ground.

Now let us transfer this comparison to mental illness versus mind control: What do we face as crude reality? The answer is a very similar comportment and result, except the poisonous snake, if left alone, does not harm anyone. As for opportunists, they are always in search of taking advantage of others' vulnerabilities to arm individuals and dupe them with false promises. The choices are clearly ours: Do we want to live in a healthy society where kindness, respect, and trust are abundant and welcomed? Or do we want to live a miserable, dictated way of life where some freedoms are allotted but everyone has to answer to a master?

Either way, mental illness versus mind control will never be compatible, just as sanity and stupidity will never be compatible. The faster we recognize the difference between exploitation and enslavement, the better we will be prepared to face these opportunists. The more time we provide to opportunists to create and pursue their dreams, the more difficult it will be to slip out of their control environment. These individuals are snakes, but if they become sneaky, it is because of support given to them on a daily basis.

The danger in interpreting mental illness occurs when natural sickness is referred to as an excuse for wrongdoing, especially when we allow a man-made agenda to create devastation. Mind control will undermine the definition of mental illness if we let mind control rule and create its own agenda, manipulated by puppeteers hidden behind the scenes.

14

DO HUMAN REPTILIANS EXIST?

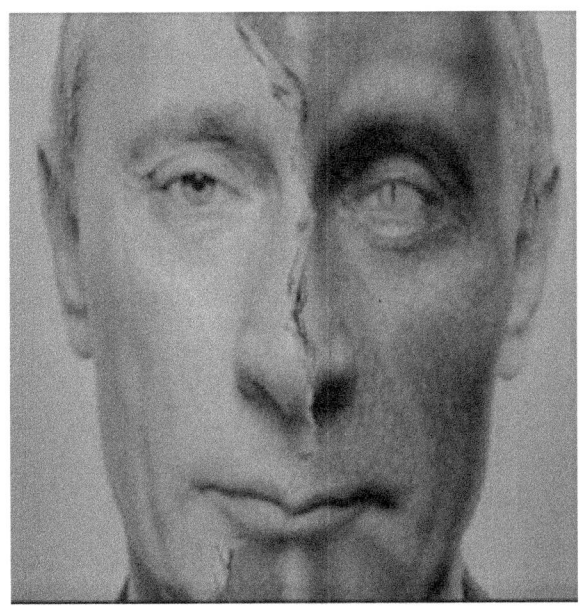

Before entering the domain of reptilian lifestyles among humans, we have to understand where and how this human condition was generated. The term "human reptilian," in my view, is another way of saying "demonic possession." I guess it is more pleasant to use human reptilian terminology than to use the real words to describe the master of deception. At least five human behaviors originate from the reptilian brain and provoke humans into mind control and hypnosis. These five behaviors are found in mind-controlling individuals:

Isocratic	Preservative
Reenactment	Deceptive
Terroristic	

These observed behaviors are used in cults and secret groups where the general public is not welcome and therefore remains ignorant.

Cultists and secret intelligence centers enable their potential victims to survive in various forms under the guise and rules of mind control after years of trial and experimentation. Cults and secret societies should not be discounted, even if they don't speak the language of the neocortex. It is important for people to know the basics about the reptilian brain because it is a part of our reality that rules without borders. There are many well-known organisms that are directly (and some indirectly) affiliated with reptilian power having taken the prestige of a good deed from another.

Now let us look further into human reptilian reality created by mind control. Mind control synchronization, using the neocortex, explores the parts of our brains that are still a great mystery to the infant "upstairs." The human reptilian brain is the most ancient of the cohesive brains. Some individuals in other religions classify the phenomenon of the human reptilian as being possessed by an impure spirit. A reptilian's brain possesses two hemispheres; it is plausible that they relate functionally to the left and right hemispheres of the neocortex. The reptilian brain consists of the upper part of the spinal cord and the basal ganglia, the diencephalon, and parts of the midbrain—all of which sit atop the spinal column like a knob in the middle of our heads.

It is very hard to labor upon the subject of a fundamental core of the nervous system without explaining the integrals facts versus discoveries made through science.

- Reptilian "high priest and its acolyte" are no longer ignorant because of their choice to follow the power of money and to explore evil knowledge to infuse itself in the knowledge of human activities where it might find expression
- Where the character and attitudes of the Illuminati come from and are revealed
- How to manipulate mentally and emotionally through television and other imagery

The basis of reptilian power and the religious ceremonies of cultists and secret societies is to acquire manipulation of the reptilian part of the human brain. The human brain will become

- obsessive with compulsive behavior
- superstitious in completing ritualistic acts

- a slave to conforming to the old ways of doing things
- engaged in ceremonial reenactments
- responsive to representations alive or inanimate
- aware of all manners in the subject of deception

Every trait generated through the reptilian brain becomes a drive to establish a will to power. A good example is a lizard's behavior when competing for dominance using ceremonial tactics that are identical but opposed to each other. These lizards have beautiful colors and use head bobbing and push-ups in assertive and aggressive courtship and greeting displays. Once engaged in a contest, the moment the gauntlet is thrown down, the aggressive displays give way to violent combat, and the struggle is unrelenting. In their victory, lizards promote mind control. They are tyrannical dictators described in a lizard manner who, during moments of war, exploit mind control. All compulsive reactions of attraction or aggression based on physical displays or representations originate in the reptilian brain. Lizards are incapable of accepting defeat; if they lose their challenge, their majestic colors soon fade, and they lapse into depression and die two weeks later.

This is a classic example we uncover when we study the path and behaviors of the Illuminati. They create in our world, and among each other, the feeling and fear of death to impose their dominant will. The mind control in forming cults and secret societies is the winning element and usually succeeds in taking it all. Are movies and television a likely projection of the reptilian brain? How do we connect movies and television to reptilian mind control?

Movies, television, and video games are all undeniably dreamlike. Not only are their presentations a symbolic reality of humans experiencing movies, but also their viewing is designed by the same brain-wave patterns as when they were dreaming. And where does dreaming originate in our head? In the reptilian brain and also in other parts of our brains connected directly and indirectly.

The film and television industry are not only controlled by reptilian bloodlines but they are created by close sources that vigilantly choose their subordinates. Illuminati individuals adhering to brotherhood are commanded and expected to honor the solemn vow they swore upon. When human reptilians gain knowledge of the secrets of mind control, the traits of their reptilian brain control them. These individuals seek to manipulate humanity through stimulation of the reptilian part of their brain. Their drive is to impose their agenda using force, and in rare cases, to exploit using kindness to give a nice picture and reputation. Obeisance is their precedent, as in legal, religious, cultural, and other aspects of the individuals who came before them.

The language of the reptilian brain is visual and constantly using multiple images. All humans becoming reptilians communicate with visual symbolic representation—each one of their movements has specific meaning. Illuminati individuals communicate with each other with secret codes to interfere with the unaware human subconscious in their endless symbolism and visual codes. It is obvious to anyone who pays attention that reptilian brains are not satisfied being relegated by the night watch of an inert body's conscience; they want far more. This illuminates the cultist structure that has propagated rituals and ceremonies, following their own theater acts on how to reach the highest level in their congregation or brotherhood.

Now where do you suppose those practices in ambiguities using structural ideologies exploiting mind control came from? It came from laboring with famous theorems, mystical invocations, human and animal sacrifices, and suppression of disbelief. This is another way of saying, "Let your left brain go to sleep while the right brain becomes reinvented in the reptilian mental state." What is repressed in reptilian individuals' waking hours secretly functions never goes to sleep due to unbalanced chemicals releasing negative neocortical. Individuals who sold themselves to become reptilians, sadly, in many cases, become the victims of reptilian evil, enabling them to function during their sleep time, even when their hemisphere becomes repressed.

Rituals in endless ceremonial deceptive theater scenes, like a movie, are created on behalf of compulsion and reaffirm a will to accentuate total power. By letting devils access mind control through film and television, our world has an excellent duplication of a reptilian mind-set, ensuring the reptilian part of the human brain to forever become a battlefield where reptilians control our reality to the point where the Earth will become infested.

Reptilians, in their sacred thirst for total power, possess a unique will to acquire power, taking in a variety of human behaviors. Behaviors and consequences of the reptilian brain:

Consume	Riot	Buy
Seek a mate	Obey	Drink
Get married	Eat	Do drugs
Breed	Kill	Hate
Reproduce	Fear	Compete
Fight	Worship	Get more
Feel guilt	Don't cooperate	Sleep
Sin	Seek differences	

The Illuminati members are obsessed with the bloodline, which is why they are using population control, famine, war, and disease to attack populations. Once an individual becomes a walking human reptilian, his territory extends far beyond a patch of earth, as his will-to-power has many masks. Once humans voluntarily become reptilian, they are actively engaged into the drive-by organisms. They are turned on and off by specific mental signals. Under any circumstance, these traffic lights or signals are to be acknowledged if they are accidently exposed to the general public. So, who's doing the driving here?

Individuals dying for power, fame, and glory connected with cults and secret societies develop disorders like compulsive reactions, attraction, and aggression based on any physical display or representation. To accept the weight of being possessed by the spirit of impulsive behavior, reptilian brains lower their body and are modified by the "higher" brain. This provokes the human reptilian brain to be a powerful source of their human behavior because it is hidden, appearing incognito at first glance. It is a deceptive, calculated entrapment to ensnare anyone and everyone in their ideologies and indoctrination exerted by speech.

Reptilian enthronement has been kept a secret from the general public. It has been well protected by the gate of fear and secrecy that allows reptilians to sneakily hide from our consciousness. If we analyze reptilians using knowledge retrieved by personal research from other warning signs, we come to discover that reptilians fall into emotionally and intuitively deceptive domains. The angel of darkness wants everyone to accept them as an angel of light, but nevertheless, they are slithering serpents full of darkness.

Subconscious possession of an evil spirit sooner or later manifests in the hidden work of the Illuminati, who have been secretly unfolding an agenda for thousands of years. Using innocent means and good causes as cover up, the Illuminati have kept the general public oblivious to its existence. Thanks to prior whistleblowers exposing degrading organizations, we have witnessed a trend in closing years of the current energy cycle where the work of the angels of darkness was subconscious and is now becoming conscious.

Pictures taken of reptilian abuses under mind control have revealed some common physical traits:

- Fake serpent teeth
- Holograms hide forms
- Serpent tongue
- Complete hologram failure
- Enlarged brow
- Wicket

It's almost like cultist and secret societies and the elite want everyone to confirm these phenomena are really happening. The more open they are in doing so, the more the magic ritual is used upon the masses of sheep. The sheep who adopt a reptilian mentality allow treacheries to take place in our society. Demon possession has no limits and no borders; it crawls like a snake into a chaotic and fractionated society. You are with us, or you are against us! I remember hearing this in a speech not too long after a major tragedy affected our country.

When it comes to the direction of a country, surely no vampires and reptilians are the ones to be blindly trusted. For some reason, sheep kept under the umbrella of reptilian mind control and vampires are free to navigate and produce their own personal agendas. Illuminati members, like cult movements, have ensnared our society without being exposed due to their audacity. I am not saying every government branch and agency is an accomplice or partner with the Illuminati.

Evidence shows us that the more openly evil people are able to function, the less attention and interrogation they have to deal with from the general public's point of view. We have been under siege and have been fooled for so many years, so now it is time for us to take charge and retrieve ourselves from imminent danger of extermination. It is time to put a stop to these bloodthirsty reptilians who benefit from knowledge on the negative level and from a destructive mind-control environment. If we allow evil to take control and guide our way of living, will we all perish?

Election after election worked specific agendas from the Illuminati. Cultist secret societies have masterly manipulated lawmakers for the governance of our country. Now more than ever, we have to engage in a direct fight against these bloodthirsty reptilians. The reptilian lifestyle is equal to demonic possession. We have been indoctrinated, and we have to step up and fight their evilness.

Mind control has become the twentieth-century calamity because it is involved in the endeavors of our own empowerment. Flashing believable lies to cover up multiple abuses imposed upon our generation and future generations is no longer excusable. An army of one divided is bound to be defeated, but an army of one united in wisdom and prudence becomes undefeatable.

These man-made religions survive only because we have been granted life today. We are here, and tomorrow will come when we will no longer be part of this Earth. Just like the founder of this massive fraudulent cult, the Illuminati, where are they to be found today? Evil perpetrates because we let evil enter our country. The fruit of evil is never relentless, but as individuals, we are not immortal.

Why do some people have so much desire to compete and fight to gain total power and control over Earth? These individuals who sold their time on Earth to become part of the reptilian rank must have noticed many inexplicable, sudden deaths. No one is immortal here on Earth; we must leave this Earth identically to the way we found it when we entered this life. However, when we saw the light of this Earth for the first time, we were naked and afraid. The day of our departure, we will have to let go of all the good we have gathered during our time allowed here on Earth.

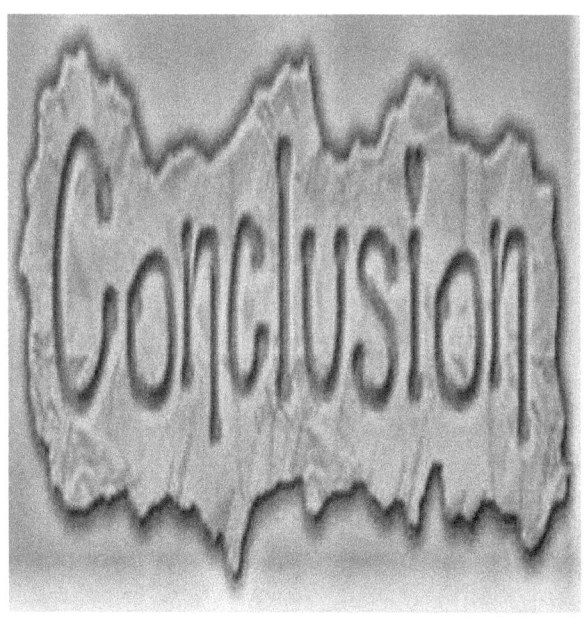

The truth is being ignored to favor a progressive agenda that is trying to defy the natural laws of perfect control over a creation set in place by the Creator. Wisdom is savagely twisted and presented in many cases, viewed by the author as tangibly suppressed in our educational system. Today, we have such a hard time recognizing any beneficial substance of prudence and autonomy. Mind control became an openly active sword used to destroy every inch of decency still existing after surviving centuries of attacks from opportunists and crooked individuals.

Where do we find a conclusion when wisdom and freedom are constantly facing attacks from the Right and Left movements? Societies seem to be kept ignorant to a hidden system or principles denied rights to applicable reasoning to any truthful branch related to knowledge and study.

Better yet, voluntary being deprived to be exposing to the ray of wisdom that investigates the principles governing correct or reliable inference. Mind control under opportunists became a particular method for reasoning. Retrieving what could work into an agenda of control tested by prior generations in a time of need is likely to portray us as unable to follow logic.

The forceful agenda took place using inexorable truths and persuasiveness incompatible with logical discoveries of all the facts. Using an established false duplicate system of principles for reasoning, historians are twisted in a specific field of study. Logic has become so twisted that it is hard to trace a straight line between what is true and how we know whether something is true. We now blindly appear to swallow branches of philosophers' analyzed patterns of reasoning by which conclusions are properly drawn. This involves formalization of logical arguments' proof in terms of symbols to represent propositions and logical connectives.

Exploitation has become the working agenda of logical connectives expressed by a set of rules that become the will of opportunists assumed to be self-evident. Rules of natural deduction describe how we may proceed from valid conclusions defining where final thoughts become expressions in predicated logic. Surely symbolic logic uses a metalanguage concerned with truth, which may or may not have a corresponding expression in the world of existence.

The modernization of symbolic logical arguments and proofs are presented in terms of historical symbols representing propositions and logical connectives. Fortunately, from vague primitives teaching functions defined admitting struggles under many difficult situations vested with precise meaning. Is mind control, under the claim of mental illness, aiming to benefit from exploitation? Crooks will write lawful passages to prove their evil took root and began with a set of rules or primitives that were assumed to be self-evident.

Mental illness predicates a self-logic that extends into existential universal quantifiers introducing bound variables ranging over finite sets taking upon values, true and false. Deduction has become a way to describe how to proceed from valid premises to certified conclusions. Mind control, in other words, became significant in logic dealing with basic operations of true values and, or, not, and some undetermined combinations thereof to predicate itself.

Logic is less concerned with what precedes thought than how it should begin to discover the truth. Logic will always be the touchstone result of thinking. Mind control versus mental illness will neither be validated as regulatory nor as a motive for its mixtures and practices in the field of exploitation. Mental illness rescuing mind control requires rational reconstructive analysis of thought or motives upon sudden craziness when they occur by motivation or by impulse.

It is apparent that no conclusion would make a subject with so much importance justified in daily manipulation and long-term devastating results. When wisdom will be restored in our society, healthy conclusions will claim victory over radical and devastating effects of impediment agendas. This would serve as the end of exploitation and lay to rest the nonsense that is negative mind control. Close, abusive systems convey surrendering puppeteers to admit statements binding the parties profiting from crooked deals due to estoppel. Collective opportunists would be barred from asserting matters such as sensible documents, fearing their corrupted inclination would commit fraudulent forgery.

Estoppel is a collective name given to a group of legal doctrines in common-law legal systems. Equitable estoppel doctrine ruled by wise judges rendering their judgment would be providing honest reasons as to why a person is prevented from exercising certain rights enacted by law. A wise system working hand in hand with wisdom will substantially overlap possessiveness and distinguish itself from the equitable doctrine of laches. Doctrines of indoctrinate into estoppel overseen by wise members in a society will relinquish certain rights once suspicions are observed and rules are applied to prevent injustice.

There are different types of estoppel that can arise from the two major sources we all encounter: the first is honesty and the other dishonesty. The common thread is that individuals are restraining to assert particular positions in law where they are judged under wisdom and are inequitable to do so. Honesty vested with wisdom and prudence regulating all estoppel results in an equitable doctrine. Accordingly, any person wishing to assert an estoppel under wisdom of logic would have to present their justifiable advances to the court with "clean hands."

How can I truly voice the power of logic? A better way to do so would be by referring to propositions concluded or inferred from the premises of an argument. This conclusion becomes the last main division of a discourse containing a summing statement from personal envisions and opinions reached. At the time, subjects expose unlawful, treacherous, surreptitious plans formulated in secret by two or more persons. Not all situations are the same, but if we follow the trail of money, soon we will discover secret plans or agreements to carry out illegal, harmful acts on the behalf of opportunists.

Crooks use multiple means and cover ups for the purpose of carrying out a combination of usurpation using unlawful secrets with evil purposes. Most of the time, mind control is used in a way to create an agreement between two or more persons to commit a crime, fraud, or other wrongful action. When vicious individual control sets a price, it usually involves a group entering into a secret agreement to achieve some illicit or harmful objective. Prices of goods usually involve duplicity and deceit aimed at achieving either personal advantages or criminal and treasonous objectives.

Most of the time, the petty intrigues of civil servants who try to investigate result in ambiguity. This conclusion is not about conspiracy of carefully planned plots or schemes; however, it exposes certain sinister ways of crooked exploitations. If we choose to act in the same self-defense as the ostrich, we risk the chance of being devoured by a slew of well-organized puppeteers with intentions to commit crimes.

Scheme in philosophy refers to a body of systems related in doctrine, pursuing theories of visionary systems of correlated ideologies. There is so much to analyze as we penetrate into the deepest of criminal intentions to do harm using innocence as a disguise. There is nothing more destructive in a society than a sentinel of parasites who viciously attack freedom to create a dictator and slavery of the people. We face insider destroyers who would never back down and are ready to eliminate any obstacle standing in their way.

There is little room left for patriotism and care for the morality and sound vitalities of good manners and consciousness. A patriot who does stand up against this new technique of mass enslavement is considered and denounced as an outsider and troublemaker. Some individuals following the footsteps of wisdom are not allowed to see the light of this Earth. This is because, according to the manipulative news, deep depression causes these individuals to fall into the pit of self-destruction by ending their own life.

Others are bumped out by snipers or found by terrorist organizations; these same individuals don't realize their own life is in jeopardy. One false movement or criticism on their behalf is waiting around the corner with a deadly sentence of guilt by knowledge. In an environment where mind control is groomed by the power of mental illness, everyone abiding by wisdom is suspected as a potential target. Therefore, as soon as rebellion starts on the behalf of wisdom, armies of hit men are put on high alert to prevent patriots from potentially taking over.

This book is not intended to play a political side, although everything points that way. I want to create a wake-up call before it's too late. Politics and mind control are avenues where if we are not well-guarded and protected, corruption and scandal bloom to the point that they will destroy the core of a nation. Hidden agendas and secrecy do not get along very well with openness and clarity found in the beneficial wonders of wisdom.

Mind control has already engulfed a majority of citizens under the many covering lies of deception, war, and indoctrination. Mental illness deficiencies serve to cover up real issues like cause and effect of brainwashing won by or forcibly imposed upon society. Systems on the governmental level have been rigged to work the agenda of opportunist puppeteers to gain more power and impose more restrictions. For centuries wisdom has been under attack, but now it seems we witness the victory of nonsense and barbaric movements gaining ground.

More than ever, we are plagued by the afflictions of wars destroying antique monuments and replacing them with desolation, emptiness, injustice, and cruelty. When will enough whispers come forward to loudly describe their society affected with an ocean of tears, suffering, anguish, hate, and above all, division? How long will this mind control invisible forces be the master of enslavement, disguising itself as peace but planting death and suffering on the inside?

I do not want to end on a sober note. Realities are relevant to global exchange of good and evil powers. This presentation is all about trying to provoke a serious awakening before we get engulfed in a cesspool of despair, hate, and dictation. Mind control and mental illness, if accepted by the general and equal public, will create a troubling time, giving perfect ground for poisonous snakes to gain control and power.

The only thing snakes know to do with precision is to crawl onto solid ground because they are slippery and unable to walk like other species. The more solid ground a snake has, the further the trajectory of its presence will be felt, but in a sneaky way. Beware of slippery, poisonous snakes that disfigure the meaning of wisdom and rampage all around our societies planting distortion, hate, division, war, and confusion. How is it possible to restore trust in a system that does everything opposite of earning respect and trustworthiness?

Individual common sense is treated as an old ideology no longer needed in modern times, which fractures the reality of previous examples where wisdom was governing. What we are witnessing is a total oblivion of equal rights and dignities under the umbrella of wisdom. This turn-around of sifted globalizations interferes with the sanity of common good to be sneakily directed toward only a few designated secret organizations or secret societies.

I can hear some of my readers screaming, "Conspiracy theory!" My question to them is why? Let's face all the facts and the pros and the cons of this before our active mind draws final conclusions. It is not because an individual becomes an active part of one organization; it becomes an immediate guarantee to escape the gate of internal retaliation. Human nature is so fragile that it is noticed in multiple individual cases of power to support one stance of ideologies, for tomorrow comes where they are confronted and gradually forced to decry their first beliefs.

While this occurs, of course, the navigation of mental illness and mind control vehicles is in full swing to distract the attention of the ones who may perceive the real face of conspiracy. Where do we find a conclusion toward totalization, a thirst for power, control, and exigency? To reach a positive ending, let us be open to ideologies of wisdom and how these strategies benefit our misguided society. Let's turn our sense to the wonders of unity, the fruit of composed virtue, and the integrity toward the knowledge of prudence and vigilance.

Like I said earlier, this book is neither blaming nor pointing a finger at anyone. It does not aim to put any legal system in its place either. It may look like I do so, but keep in mind, if it does, it means something needs to be rectified. Let's give the benefit of wisdom to eradicate once and for all the seed of deception and division. Let us, with the help of public servants, restore faith and trust in the judicial system that gives us opportunities to heal wounds caused by injustices. It's never too late to rectify a wrong, but if we let it be, it becomes harder to straighten out the consequences and destructions of these avenues.

I don't want to end my presentation on mind control and its effects in a negative way because there is much more we can create out of this than desolation. It is a question of a will to create a situation where wrongdoing has been rectified. Amendments are needed in order to start a new beginning, a fresh start based upon common natural laws of wisdom that bring prosperity. Together, united by the flame of creativity, resulting from wisdom in our society, we are in a position to claim victory over evil, including all its ambiguities.

Remember, we reap what we sow, and yesterday becomes the prelude of tomorrow. The day after tomorrow becomes the continuation of the next generation. Evil forces are only strong and active when we give them the power over circumstance to open the gate of national laws and regulations. Gatekeepers are needed more than ever because the attack on evil is so sophisticated in our day. Why do we have to endure such desolation, division, and discontent?

Nothing binds us to evil; we are the ones who bind our future and the future generations to evil and desolation. It is becoming a matter of responsibility and pride to be able to sustain sophisticated attacks imposed on us on behalf of pure evil. We have opportunities to make the right choices and to create dire consequences to anyone breaching the laws of wisdom and common sense.

As we progress in the field of wisdom, we will be able to discern ahead of time the enemy's plan, whose only goals are to plant despair, discordance, and hate. We would be in a position to take challenges and prepare to be challenged in how strongly we are anchored to our principles and beliefs. A wise man alone could possibly defeat his worst enemy, but an idiot who never paid attention to wisdom makes the perfect ground to be destroyed at first strike.

Not all mind control is a bad thing because there have to be forms of control governing society. I do not want anyone to think I am against mind control and its effects. Far from it. I recognize the need for mind control, but I object to the abuse of power we have in the vast field of mind control. At the end of the day, it does not matter what others think about. What matters is the disposition and the willingness to positively progress in a decent society.

We, as a core, have the choice to render ourselves and reflect upon our future generations. We take an oath to our future generations—what we consider beneficial wisdom and the healthy meaning of conducting our affairs. Let us be equitable toward younger generations by giving them good examples of dignity and pride; let us give them prosperity instead of misfortune. We will be recognized by the way we choose to live our destinies while we give opportunities to take monetary advantages or to solidify fundamentals for our future generations.

I will end my presentation with this question: Can we honestly justify an abusive system operating under the cover of mind control by a misrepresentation of mental illness? The answer belongs to each one of us, but the result is not for us to be the judge. Future generations will become our judges in casting their equitable sentencing. As they pronounce their sentencing upon our commitment, we will not be able to repeal any positive or negative consequences of our actions.

The time for action is now. Tomorrow is not a guarantee to any of us, and yesterday cannot be changed in the course and consequences of personal choice. We have to stand by our principles and remember every day that what we can achieve today might not make it happen tomorrow. The present moment is the only moment we have to care about and respond to.

Accountability versus negligence will always be adversary because no one is able to be in two camps at the same time. We have to stand by the production of our diligence or disqualification of our negligence as to who will become our inequitable judge. Future generations of judgment will be provided in light of the evidence of our enthusiasm or our lack of motivation. Personal accountability encompasses all phases of the life process, and before the action is deliberate during the assessment of the results and after we have passed away.

Accountability is the key notion we discover about responsibilities entrusted to us at birth. Accountability can reflect positive or negative consequences in terms of three questions: (1) What resources were entrusted? (2) What have we produced? (3) What are the outcomes?

Throughout the entire process of our life, we must be willing to take personal ownership for (1) understanding and accepting discipline, (2) taking full responsibility and accountability, and (3) answering any invitations to follow wisdom. Personal accountability focuses on the outcomes, which are, at the end of our time here on Earth, a glorious or lamentable daily process. One day at a time provides the opportunity to become noble individuals; it also provides opportunities to rattle and idle while we are given occasion for everyone to accentuate. The outcome for each individual is measured by that person's efforts and willingness to face the consequences of personal choice, whether he or she succeeds in achieving a career or chooses to become a major failure.

Intimidations and provocations serve to develop the characteristics of individuals who are self-confident, destroying forever the ones who nonchalantly gobble everything, grasping thin air for their survival.